5/1/73

To Andrea,

You, I am sure,
are never guilty of
any of these in
your therapy.

Bill

MARTIN SHEPARD, M.D.,
and MARJORIE LEE

G. P. Putnam's Sons, New York

Games Analysts Play

GAMES ANALYSTS PLAY

TO PEOPLE

Preface

ALTHOUGH the games described in this book were created by psychoanalysts, and are played chiefly by them, other categories of counselors and mental health workers may be found employing similar techniques. In order that the game-playing field not seem restricted to analysts alone, the letter *T* is used to include therapists of varying ranks.

The authors wish to express their gratitude to the following people for their influence or their actual help:

Eivor Shepard; Marc and Richard Shepard; Marcia and Mac Shepard; Helen Edey; Lee Arima; Roberta and Melvin Grossgold; Ralph and Mary Crowley; Edward Tauber; Harry Bone; Stuart Miller; Albert Ellis; William Schutz; Robert S. Lee, Sr.; Elaine K. G. Benson; Barbara Norville; Anne Tiffany; Rita P. Dogole; Max Gartenberg.

Contents

Introduction

THIS book is written in the belief that it is beneficial for both patients and therapists to be reminded that those in charge of directing, molding, and healing the human psyche are themselves human and therefore fallible.

There are today in the United States some three-quarters of a million persons who earn their livelihood by ministering to the emotionally troubled. A conservative estimate of the number of people they treat (assuming each therapist sees twenty patients a week) leads to the fact that there are more than fifteen million Americans who are working *at any one time* with mental health professionals. There are few families in our nation who have not had one member or another in treatment. Yet in spite of the enormous amounts of money spent and the countless hours passed in expressing personal unhappiness, there is, far too often, little to show for the investment.

Who are these people who deal with our suffering? How well are they trained? What are they like as individuals? *What are the rationales behind their methods of treatment?*

These are the questions which most patients never think of asking; and if they do, they are all too frequently met with the rejoinder: "Why do you ask?" This very response often contains the answer within it: It can indicate that the therapist is an excessive game-player—someone who is afraid to reveal the person behind the professional façade, someone who would rather joust verbally than deal directly with these very vital and pertinent issues.

Yet there *is* great variety among therapists in terms of both quality and technique. The best-known technique is classical Freudian analysis. Here the patient is expected to see the analyst four or five times a week for several years. He lies down on a couch, says anything that comes into his mind, and deals with a therapist who does his best to remain strictly neutral so as not to influence his patient's verbal productions. Eventually all this random talk is expected to coalesce into patterns of interest and concern; hidden thoughts and attitudes will emerge, and this emergence is expected to cure.

Those therapists influenced by the Neo-Freudian analysts, such as Harry Stack Sullivan, Karen Horney, Alfred Adler, and Erich Fromm, often meet with their patients less frequently (two to three times a week), and face to face. The therapist allows himself to respond more actively to what his patient says, feeling that by sharing his knowledge, ideas, and concerns he can hasten the therapeutic process. He becomes a participant-observer rather than simply an observer.

Rogerian "client-centered" therapists also emphasize talking treatment, and again usually have their patients (called "clients" in an attempt not to degrade those they see by presuming them to be ill) sit rather than lie down. They allow themselves to participate more than a Freudian would, yet less than the Neo-Freudians—in that they limit their remarks to restating whatever it was that their client has just said. They feel that such re-summations promote growth by heightening the client's sense of his situation, thus making it harder for him to avoid coming to grips with his conflicts.

Then there are those therapists descended from Wilhelm

Reich, who approach people's problems by working on the tensions in their bodies through exercises. An overly docile patient may be encouraged to hit a pillow and shout in the hope that he will rediscover his hidden anger in the process. Or a politely negativistic type may be encouraged to flail away with arms and legs while lying down, yelling "I won't!" The hope here would be to let the person get a fuller sense of his underlying emotional attitudes.

Still other therapists have been influenced by the "here and now" approaches pioneered by Fritz Perls (Gestalt Therapy) and other leading "Experientialists" such as William Schutz. Most of these techniques are utilized in groups, and are the subject of another book. Briefly stated, their approaches are intended to give the patient a new experience, and their feelings seem to be that man is not limited by what he knows, but rather by what he has yet to learn and experience.

Many people choose their therapists without realizing the variety available. A friend suggests they "see Dr. Smith who did such marvelous work with my cousin" or "with me." In some cases they are referred to the only therapist known personally to their family physician. In others, they are assigned a therapist in the local clinic. Whether the therapist is a Freudian, Sullivanian, Rogerian, Horneyan, or any other kind of *ian* is rarely clarified. Indeed, whether the analyst is a psychoanalyst, psychiatrist, psychologist, or social worker is often not known. The patient at the onset of treatment is a creature of vast uncertainty; for him it is any port in a storm, and he dare not make waves.

An exhaustive examination of the underlying assumptions, conceptual framework, and techniques of the healing art from a historical perspective would unquestionably aid the reader to grasp where psychotherapies are at this time. Such a task is impossible to accomplish within the confines of this book. Suffice it to say that regardless of the theoretical house in which any particular therapist worships, the biggest point of contention is between those therapists who emphasize talking-and-understanding (the "classical analysts") and those who emphasize acting-and-experiencing ("encounter"). These are the polarities, the two extremes. Most therapists today combine both approaches, to varying degrees. Too often, however, the balance is tipped heavily in favor of the intellectual and verbal approach, so profound has been the influence of classical theory in the psychological and psychiatric training centers of this country.

We believe that this imbalance operates to the detriment of patients. (See Part III: A Theory of Change.) It recalls the story of a thirty-five-year-old patient of Freud who was a bed-wetter. Seven years of treatment having passed, he was approached by a friend who asked, "How's the analysis coming?"

Patient: Wonderful. Very helpful indeed.

Friend: Have you stopped wetting the bed?

Patient: No. But now I know why I do it.

Those who are concerned with psychotherapy have begun slowly to recognize that the effort to maintain a neutral, non-judgmental therapeutic atmosphere—valuable and even imperative in many respects—can create problems, foreseeable only after the ill effects have occurred. The major psychotherapists, beginning with Freud, appreciated the importance of uncontaminated intervention by the therapist. Later came the empirical discovery that the very lack of "contamination" called forth a sterility between healer and patient, thus defeating a core ingredient of therapy: an authentic encounter.

We have attempted to point out how the therapeutic orientation has often unwittingly interfered with the very aims of its healing intent. Simplification is unavoidable here, yet we trust that by dramatizing the issues through game-analysis we can make up for the impracticality of a lengthier, more scholarly exposition of these limitations. This book aims to sharpen uncompromisingly the boundaries of our shared foibles, insensitivities, and theoretical fallibilities.

As therapists, we can all afford at this late date in psychiatric history to focus on our own games. We can afford to permit our patients to challenge us, question us, and discover our common humanity. Such challenges should help keep us on our toes, to grow as we expect our patients to grow, and to be more effective.

What is "funny" in this book should evoke our laughter, as well as our patients' laughter, without, we hope, failing to convey to our readers our aim to broaden the horizon of hope for those who seek help.

M. S.
M. L.

PART I
Definitions

*We are all more simply human
than otherwise.*

HARRY STACK SULLIVAN

Chapter 1
Being Human

THE challenge implicit in a humanizing view of any therapist is self-evident. Humanization is difficult because therapists have worked so hard at being, or seeming to be, inhumanly nice—in a more total sense, "above it all." This is the result of an unchallenged acceptance of the theory of positive transference, as elaborated by Freud.

In truth, a patient will regard his therapist positively if he receives help from him. It may take a while before the patient is in any psychological position to recognize help for what it is; he will go through phases of denial, with an absence of recognition of the good work being done. But the therapist who does help will in time come through with a positive transference from his patient.

Absurdly, however, many therapists attempt to structure the transference, and this conscious (and unconscious) attempt to build respect and admiration prevents the patient from exploring other feelings which are, in the body of the work, far more essential. The therapist who deliberately structures the analytic relationship is, in fact, acting upon a theoretical delusion, or disguised narcissism; and the patient responds accordingly. Thus, reality, which is the basic goal of all therapy, is either obfuscated or lost.

The very nature of most therapeutic relationships enhances this fantasy. The therapist adopts a role of "neutrality" or "total acceptance" in relation to the patient. The patient

19

reveals his hang-ups, but the therapist will not reciprocate. And so, to the troubled patient, the therapist continues to appear phenomenally serene and invulnerable.

For the therapist, however, an awareness of his own subjectivity, and his freedom to display it, requires a degree of courage and conviction almost equal to the efforts which the patient must make on *his* behalf. To begin with, the therapist was, at one time, the patient of another therapist; and the chances are good that this original therapist did little to reveal his own full range of emotions. Indeed, it is considered axiomatic at most psychotherapeutic training centers (residency programs, psychoanalytic institutes, post-graduate schools) that angry, jealous, or sexual reactions on the part of the therapist are subhuman; such reactions are immediately labeled *countertransference,* and the assumption is that the exhibitor of this behavior is neurotic. Small wonder that so many trained and practicing therapists lose contact with their own emotionality, attempt to deny it, and readily retreat behind masks of coolness, benignancy, detachment, or strict neutrality. And smaller wonder that, in replacement for what might be a direct form of helpfulness, they resort to games. It is their very spontaneity that could be most directly beneficial; yet it is this same spontaneity that is stifled both in the therapist's training and in the interests of building a *positive transference.*

One of the most potent tools any therapist possesses is his ability to serve as a "role model." How free can the patient be to reveal his "shameful" emotionality if the godlike therapist shows none of his own? A therapist who is unashamed and comfortable enough to show his anger and sexuality helps the patient to feel more at ease and less ashamed of these same traits.

As is true of the majority of people one knows, most therapists are decent human beings. But to be human also means to be imperfect. There is beauty and banality in all of us. We are domineering and ill-tempered, as well as tender and loving. We talk of selflessness, but we are quite ambitious. We are concerned about the underprivileged, yet we charge fees which few underprivileged people can afford. We admire humility, but often we fall prey to vanity. We profess to be open and honest; at the same time we are hypocrites. We are loved by some and despised by others, and we return these feelings, each for each, out of the need for fairness and equality borne within our own egos. We are alternately bored and enthused by things and people. We try hard to respect the other fellow's autonomy, but all too frequently we assume that we "know best."

One of the most persistent traits of the psychiatric patient is his enormous self-doubt. He is unsure of his own worth; he lacks faith in his instincts. He fears that his particular set of emotions makes him subhuman. He has spent the better part of his life attempting to keep them hidden. Among these hidden emotions are his sexuality, aggressivity, boredom, uninterest, and irritability. Coexistent is a fear of spontaneity, an awareness of the dangers of making a fool of himself by exposing his secrets. Being down, he looks up. He tends, even before the onset of the analytic relationship, to make gods of other men—an emotional error which serves only to perpetuate his low self-esteem. And if a god-man or a god-woman does exist for him, he seeks revelations from this object rather than turning inward to find the answers for himself. In this way he elaborates upon his subservient position. He is the mortal in relation to the god, or the child in relation to the parent. *Feed me,* he says or feels; *take care of me; love me. And, in return, I will worship you.*

In any successful therapy, a patient will sooner or later be able to eliminate his neurotic self-doubt. Many patients actually do have good relationships with their therapists, and depart with a respectful fondness. Others, however, must work hard and long before achieving a position of equality. Some never do.

This battle, in its developmental stages, is quite apparent in the newly emancipated ex-analysand who may remark lightly and with a certain flair, "Well, I guess the bastard helped me after all"—or, closer to the bone of such thinly coated hostility, "Look, I've had it. He was every bit as sick as I was." One ex-analysand, survivor of several separate bouts for salvation, urged herself along the path to equality and collected the additional regard of her friends' applause by saying, "I've paid for five trips to the Riviera for those birds. Now I'm going myself!"

Hostility, yes; but in some cases it is a hostility used in the service of going free. For it is not easy to beat out the ploys of a master-player. Along with the pain of self-exploration there is the blissful comfort of the therapeutic womb: the dimly lit office in which one finally lies down in the knowledge and trust that a veritable god will listen, love, take care of. *I lied when I was little . . . I broke my sister's favorite toy . . . I masturbated . . . I stole a bag of marbles from the Five and Ten . . . I hated my mother. . . .* And no sharp slap ensues, no condemnation, no punishment; nothing worse, in fact, than Hhmmnn. (See *Hhmmnn:* Games.)

Sooner or later, however, neither the Hhmmnn nor its related devices will be needed. Hopefully, the day, the year, will come when all external approval or nondisapproval game-props will be cast out and replaced by the patient's own, "So I did it. So what. So that's *me*."

The question is: what day, what year?

Unfortunately, many treatment situations founder on the rocks of the Pedestal Syndrome. The patient elevates the therapist to a godly position, as has been stated. The therapist enjoys such flattery (particularly in its more subtle forms) and does little to destroy the illusion. Even if the therapist does make an attempt to lower his lofty niche somewhat, the patient refuses to believe it. He will assume that it is modesty on the part of the therapist, which serves only to elevate the pedestal another foot or two.

The patient who is deeply entangled in the therapist's unconscious need to be iconized will spend an endless amount of time and money before the introduction of any workable reality in his therapy or life. Games of analysis lasting twenty years are by no means unheard of. Those covering four and five years are practically par for the course. There is the gag these days that anybody who has not undergone a complete second analysis is nobody at all. In the case of these second-rounders, the therapist is in a fortunate position. He is the one who can afford to indulge in *Off the Record* and *I'll Be Frank with You,* thereby undoing and abolishing the first therapist's position. He is able to make an entrance into the arena in the fresh white garb of the True Human Being, which, because of its double reward, often turns out to be the best game-opportunity of all. The loose ends of the previous analysis are wrapped up, the entangling cords are cut, and both the therapist and the patient emerge successful.

Chapter 2
A Definition of Analysts

IN the strictest sense, a psychoanalyst is someone who has gone through medical school, taken a year of medical internship, spent three years working in a mental hospital as a psychiatric resident, and has undergone five or more years of psychoanalytic training and an actual analysis of his own. This training means that of all those people practicing psychotherapy, the psychoanalyst has acquired, by virtue of the time spent in studying the field, the most prestige.

Our definition of the word "analyst," however, is more inclusive. It consists of all those professional people who meet with emotionally troubled individuals and try to help them. This, too, is invariably the patient's definition of analyst. Whether the therapist seen is a social worker, a psychologist, a physician, or a psychoanalyst, to the patient he is always My Analyst. For being treated by an analyst connotes being treated by the most prestigious therapist in the field.

Analysis carries such a high note of prestige, as opposed to other forms of therapy, or forms of therapy which merely have other names, that therapists themselves play oneupmanship games with the term. One well-known psychoanalyst, when asked by another analyst what the actual difference was between analysis and therapy, quipped, "Analysis is what *I* do; therapy is what *you* do."

The tendency of patients, then, to call their therapists analysts comes not only from the patients' desire to have "the very best," but also from many therapists' attempt to inflate their limited training and to patch up a sense of inadequacy and inferiority. The college graduate employed as a social worker, who decides to set up a private practice and has read Freud's *Interpretation of Dreams,* will often be the first to describe himself as an analyst.

Therapists come from everywhere, and have different ranks according to educational backgrounds. They have been trained in social work schools, graduate schools in psychology, psychiatric residency training programs, and psychoanalytic institutes. Yet approximately only one out of every hundred therapists has undergone the full and arduous climb to the top rank of professional psychoanalyst. While the works of Freud and his followers hold influential sway in nearly all training programs, long training is often cut short, and degrees, diplomas, or certificates are given to those who have done little more than scratch the surface of the psychoanalytic field.

In the United States we have 2,500 orthodox Freudian analysts and analysts in training, about 1,000 neo-Freudians (followers of Sullivan, Horney, Adler, and others), approximately 25,000 psychiatrists in practice or in training, 34,000 psychologists, and 375,000 social workers. The best estimate of the number of psychologists and social workers who administer some form of treatment (psychotherapy, group work, case work, counseling, family or marital therapy, etc.) as opposed to administration, teaching, research, personnel work, or testing is 55 percent. Thus there is an approximate grand total of one-quarter of a million working "analysts" in the country at the present time; and we have not even begun to tabulate therapists operating in self-help groups such as Alcoholics Anonymous, Synanon, Schizophrenics Anonymous, and so forth—plus psychiatric nurses, religious counselors, school guidance counselors, progressive school dons.

Nor have we included the increasing number of therapists being trained in Encounter work at Growth Centers, such as Esalen, which are quickly springing up around the country.

There are few fields as attractive to a well-educated, sensitive, and neurotic individual as the psychological sciences. He can study the intricacies of the mind, and obtain solace without having to go through the imagined humiliations of publicly acknowledging his own psychological difficulties; to boot, at a later stage of training, such acknowledgment becomes the mature and In thing to do. Surrounded by a small coterie of colleagues, he cements the bonds of friendship by sharing personal foibles.

While the bulk of training for any therapist is picked up with the supervisor and the candidate's personal analyst, some comments on formal classroom training are in order: The candidate learns about the history of the analytic movement, and the lives of those giants who furthered it. He discovers that this immense analytic tent can house many (some might say any) points of view. He may choose his prophet in accordance with his own preferences and point to a written body of expert opinion to justify his way of seeing things. He learns, too, that the lives of these great men were inseparably joined to their theories, and that these theories arose from their own troubled backgrounds and were then applied universally to all men. Freud, for example, had a very special relationship with his mother, and formulated the Oedipal Triangle theory. Sullivan, never having had a special relationship with anyone, stressed, instead, the importance of interpersonal relations.

The therapeutic candidate learns of the irrevocability of early development: that having a mother inevitably means trouble, and that being toilet-trained compounds it. He learns that dreams are essential to personal understanding, and that they can be interpreted in as myriad ways as there are numbers of dreamers and interpreters; and that no one, therefore, can invalidate *his* interpretation.

He learns from his peers, and from small talk with teachers, some of the unwritten rules governing social customs among therapists. For example:

1. Take a month off every summer, preferably in August. The break is needed in such emotionally exhausting work, and it is also good for the patients who get a chance to operate and live things through independently.
2. Vacations spent on the Cape or in the Hamptons carry a certain snob-appeal which is in no way detrimental. (We speak now of East Coast analysts; West Coasters have haunts of their own. In-places, currently, are Carmel, Puget Sound, Big Sur, Las Vegas, Laguna Beach.)
3. The number of articles and books written and the number of papers presented orally (as opposed to the number of patients handled in therapy) enhances standing and reputation in the analytic and social community.
4. There is also enhancement in the cultivation of some special avocational interest or hobby. Playing with a string quartet or jazz combo, wine-tasting, collecting etchings or paintings adds a depth to the personality and proves that shop-talk is not constantly essential.
5. Marriage and children are preferable; divorce causes a stir, but it is accepted as a mature and self-aggrandizing move when it is followed, at some reasonable point, with remarriage.

In toto, the candidate, or trainee, learns what it means to be an expert. His models include his teachers, his supervisor, and his analyst. A supervisor is a person who monitors the future therapist's handling of patients at the beginning of his own practice. In other words, the candidate treats his own patient and then reports to the supervisor about what has transpired. The supervisor tells him "how to do it better." The candidate's analyst is the person whom the trainee sees several times a week in order to talk of his own problems.

To become an expert means, essentially, to be thought one by all superiors and by the public. To satisfy the former, the future therapist must go through a proscribed period of training, attend dutifully to his instructors, and impress them sufficiently with his stability and "openness" to warrant certification. To satisfy the latter, he must learn to talk like an expert, act like an expert, and charge like an expert.

An expert rarely speaks in a language which can be readily understood by the ordinary man. If he sounds like everybody else, his patients lose faith in him and wonder why they are paying upwards of $25 an hour. Why not, in that case, simply call up a good friend? So the first step, usually taken during the course of residence training, is, unfortunately, to master the knack of translating the simple into the complex. The general rule is never to call a spade a spade if it can be called an implement for the transportation of terra firma. (See *Big Words:* Games.)

The supervision part of training is often quite an ordeal, for dealing with a supervisor is akin to dealing with a Jewish Mother. The supervisor (S) must make the Candidate (C) realize that C doesn't have all the answers, that S knows best, that he expects C to follow his suggestions, and that there are always better ways of doing things. S will not accept what C does at face value; it is important to let C know that he cannot squeak by without S.

Here are some of the basic rules which are followed by S in his training of C:

1. Never admit that C has done a better job than S could have done.

2. Always leave C with the thought that there is a little more to be done.

3. Whenever things are chaotic, make C feel that clarity might have resulted for the patient if C had only asked the right question. The "right question" is often a thing of sensitivity and subtlety. For example: C reports a case in which an apparently happily married woman has suddenly turned against her husband, openly initiated an affair with another man, and started to smoke. S finds that C has asked all the relevant questions and has gathered reams of information, but that none of it sheds real light on the woman's current activities. S must then ask for material which C has failed to unearth and for which he has no answer, such as: "Do you know what she felt about her dinner last night?" or "What brand of cigarettes is she smoking?"

The purpose of C's personal analysis is not only to establish a quality control—that is, to help him to become a healthier person—but to instill in him great confidence in his craft. Such faith is necessary to carry him through the number of therapeutic failures or marginal successes which he will experience in the future. And there is no better way to become convinced than by seeing proof-positive changes while being a patient himself. The candidate's analyst (CA) teaches C three basic things:

1. It is healthy to know that you are unhealthy.
2. You can always dig deeper.
3. If two years are good, four years are better.

The idea behind all this is that C can never have too much treatment; he will be singularly fortunate if he has enough.

It is customary for CA to charge a stiff fee. The unself-conscious stating of a high fee for CA from C lessens C's shame and guilt about the high fees he himself will ultimately be charging. In fact, C must charge these fees in order to keep up with his payments of CA's fees, S's fees, and if he is already married, the fees of his wife's analyst. Particularly among psychoanalysts, unanalyzed wives are *de trop*. The very thought of having such a wife would be as socially devastating as spending vacations on Coney Island.

C's challenge is to find his way to health. Should he by any chance dare, with S or CA, to presume health prematurely, he is brought up short with the old saw that "Everyone has problems, so what are you trying to deny?" Yet the acknowledgment of problems will not buy a certificate of health either, because "if you've got problems, then isn't it healthier to stay and work them out?" The logic is inescapable; the treatment proceeds.

No matter how many ways in which a living situation is analyzed, there is yet another level of analysis possible. CA needs only to ask C "Why?" or "What do you make of that?" These questions can be used on C for any and all circumstances. For instance: C keeps telling CA of an intense dislike for one of his supervisors—a Dr. Brown. After several weeks of probing why-questions, he comes to a session with the following dream: *I went to Dr. Brown's office and there he was, sitting in a strangely familiar overstuffed armchair, eating chocolate bonbons, conveying them to his mouth with his pinkie extended . . . and on the pinkie was a large zircon ring.* CA, knowing that Dr. Brown never munches chocolates in his office, and has no such ring or armchair, inquires as to whom C might really be dreaming of. Suddenly the Eureka Phenomenon occurs. C leaps up and shouts, "Uncle Joe, that old sonuvabitch!" And sure enough, the good uncle, long since deceased, was hooked on gooey chocolates, and possessed just such a ring and armchair. And was despised. But will that be enough to account for C's dislike of Dr. Brown? No. This is only the first year of training analysis. Rather than allow smug satisfaction to turn the head of the neophyte, CA counters with, "And what do you make of that?" Indeed, a good deal *can* be made of it. Why was Uncle Joe the object of a negative transference? For whom was Uncle a misplaced surrogate?

The idea that one can never get enough of a good thing is gotten across by the value scales applied to the length of training analysis:

1. Three years or less   Incomplete analysis
2. Six years or more   Difficult analysis
3. Three to six years   Thorough analysis

The optimum number of years for a Thorough Analysis depends, actually, upon the policies of the school or center at which the candidate trains.

Regardless of the school, at some point past the third year, the CA stops asking "Why?" or "What do you make of that?" and, by his silence, tacitly accepts what C says at face value. C, at first unnerved by this, gradually comes to believe that he has some answers, feels increasingly healthy and self-confident, has the idea that he has won CA's respect, and terminates. He has seen treatment work. He, as well as CA, has profited by it.

And so, several years from the day of beginning his training as a therapist, graduation occurs and a new *analyst* is launched upon the world. He has been bombarded by so many divergent dicta during his development that unless he is very careful he will lose sight of the forest for the trees. He

order to avoid thinking it out altogether, a number is placed after a written phrase or paragraph. This number corresponds, at either the bottom of the page or at the end of the chapter or book, to the name of the man who said it first, and to the title of his book. In the reading of most psychiatric material, the layman finds that he has been turned over to [1]Freud, [2]Spitz, [3]Rank, and [4]Klein, and that until he understands these sources, he will not understand the theory.

A fourth game is Literary Quotations, in which Shakespeare and the Bible figure first and foremost as pawns. "Sufficient unto the day is the evil thereof" is widely used and means very little to most people.

A fifth is a game which will be further described in this book: *Big Words*. Words are, actually, the best way of communicating definitions, but it will be found that little ones do the job in a fraction of the time.

What is a game? Here are some dictionary definitions:

1. A sport of any kind; fun.
2. An amusement or diversion.
3. A scheme; plan; project.
4. A contest, physical or mental, according to set rules, undertaken for amusement or for stakes.

Since the advent of books and treatises on games and gamesmanship, we have learned to invest the term with more abstract qualities of meaning.

In the course of one day and night we "play" with each human being we know, talk to, or even simply see. We play with those closest to us, and with those whom we pass in the street. To merely glance at a stranger in passing is a contact game. To walk by without looking at all is a denial-of-contact game. Both are moves made in the service of relating—either toward or away from.

Alone, we sigh, hum, sing, grimace, utter secret sounds,

speak aloud, or just think. These are self-relating games, or games in which we seek and perpetuate contact with the self. Dreams are self-relating games. The fantasy, or daydream, is a mental and emotional play, enacted on the inner stage for the audience of self. Night-dreams, in sleep, are messages from our selves, sent to our selves, up through the most hidden areas of the psyche to a level on which, if they are not understood, they may at least be "remembered." Night-dreams are the pursuits for contact between our covert selves and our overt selves.

The "things" in our lives are often used as props on the emotional game-board, as are checkers and chessmen. They are inanimate objects which we employ as human-object substitutes. Take the telephone: We use it as a means of communication in order to facilitate a human-contact situation; yet we are also capable of playing games with the telephone itself. When waiting for an important call which may relay good or loving news, we say, or think, or feel, "Please ring. I'll count to fifty slowly; I'll read twenty pages of this book in my lap; I'll tidy up this room. Before I'm finished, you'll ring." Here the telephone itself becomes the second player. Another example might be makeup: A woman, preparing for a date or a party, uses her cosmetics as a contact line for a game with those whom she wishes to impress. At the same time she may, while looking into the mirror, say, think, or feel, "Please let me look great tonight." In this instance the thought is not simply a prayer to God or to herself for this reward; it is a plea to her lipstick and her mascara-brush to work, to come through for her. These two objects have now become her second and third prayers; and the word *please* is a ploy, meant to evoke sympathetic reaction.

There is need to emphasize the total everythingness of mes. Owing to dictionary definitions, by which we have been indoctrinated, we tend to believe that games, even when played emotionally, are sport. Recently we have learned that this sport can be dangerous or "bad." While we have an awareness that some games do pay off, and can therefore be thought of as "good," we are still relegating game-life to a concept of false play. We must expand our understanding to the point where we can recognize the fact that games *are* life; that games are not constructions, but exist in nature.

Here are two very simple games:

I. Two people meet, as one is entering a restaurant and one is exiting:

    A: Hi.

    B: Oh, hi there!

    A: Haven't seen you for ages, must be a year.

    B: Brown's. Harry Brown's house.

    A: Him either. Where've you been?

    B: Around, busy, you know.

    A: Get together.

    B: Like that a lot, call you.

    (A begins to move out. B responds, also moving.)

    B: Week or so, okay? Best to Janet!

    A: Thanks. And Joannie!

II. Two people at home, or on a date:

    C: I want to talk to you.

    D: Yes?

    C: Look at me.

    D: I'm looking.

    C: You never look at me when I talk anymore.

    D: Oh, come on.

    C: Whaddya mean, come on!

    D: I mean talk.

    C: What's the point in talking, you don't listen to me.

Game I is benign. It might be called *I'm Nice, You're Nice.* A says "Hi," beginning a contact; B mentions a mutual friend, making a common bond. This is later added to by the use of their wives' first names. Probably A and B will not "get together," but no harm has been done, and the pay-off will be a memory of pleasantness, perhaps functional in the future.

In Game II, or *Heads I Win, Tails You Lose,* C manipulates D into a position where he is unable to play. This is a hostile game, and, as in all hostile games, both players fail. It can be said that C wishes to fail, and in failing, wins; but this is a reverse-win and is, ultimately, a loss in that it may eventually lead to a total break in contact.

Neither game is "good" or "bad" so much as a facet of nature. One is simply pleasant, while the other is sad and unrewarding. Yet, these days, we tend to feel that the reminder that a game is being played is, in fact, a kind of criticism. Since the publication of Dr. Eric Berne's book (*Games People Play*), we are quick to point out to others that they are playing; but we mean by that that something neurotic, or not quite cricket, or downright underhanded is going on. We are implying that if these people were only nice enough, or astute enough, they would see the folly of their ways and be "better." And they, in return, respond to the implied admonition with feelings of discomfort or anger.

We labor under the misapprehension that games are not real. There is an intrinsic connotation of staginess which evokes associations of costumes, greasepaint and other false accoutrements: again, the mistake of the "sport" concept. The word *playing* has a ring of duplicity. Yet the play and interplay of human relationship belongs, in both figurative and literal senses, to a "living" theater. We are not acting. We are being.

It is here that the psychotherapist and his many and varied

counterparts come in: for those who have grasped the meaning of games-as-life, there is still that last barrier to be vaulted—the unconscious belief, even in those who are knowledgeable and sophisticated, that even though games are the breathing machinery of the common man, there are others belonging to some superhuman tribe who are above being drawn in or affected. Is it possible that the men and women who are, allegedly, the masterminds of emotional cause and effect find themselves incapable of staying out of the arena? The answer should be clear: If that arena is life, and if life is reality, only dead men and plaster icons are exempt. One does not pay fees to a dead man, except in memory or in guilt. One does, in several instances, pay fees to plaster icons. But it is a disservice to therapists to rob them, ideologically, of their flesh-and-blood properties. And it is an equal disservice for therapists to perpetuate the myth of their unreality within their patients. To do so is to turn the constructive game of *Help* into a wasteful travesty.

The question now is to differentiate those games which are the essence of life from those which are intellectually and emotionally constructed for the purpose of delusion—both a delusion for those who are playing and for those who are being played upon.

Since life is a series of transactions between and among people, and since every transaction can be considered a game, life itself must be seen as one. Yet such a definition is so broad that one book based on the games analysts play would never suffice. Indeed, a continuously appended encyclopedia would be more in order to cover every pattern of interaction, both positive and negative, that might be played out in the therapist's office.

One game, in this broadest sense, is, as has been pointed out, the Definition Game itself. The rules here indicate that a thing is whatever you choose to call it. Thus, all furry quadrupeds that bark may be defined as dogs. On the other hand, going up the scale to include more things in this category, they may be defined as mammals also. Or to cut down on the number of things involved, they may be defined as cocker spaniels.

Since our aim in this book is to take a critical look at some of the unfruitful games which psychotherapists initiate, we shall take full advantage of the Definition Game to define our chosen games as *unproductive transactions.*

Our premise, then, is that games exist whenever the therapist's behavior (in word, deed, or silence) is employed to disguise his true feelings. It is for this reason that we have categorized our games according to feelings or attitudes which the therapist is trying to deny, or to hide from his patient: his boredom, lust, tenderness, rage, etc.

Games which are deliberately constructed are, at best, unproductive. At worst, they are extremely harmful. They dehumanize the therapist in the eyes of the patient, thereby replacing the real help-object with an untouchable and unreachable automaton. This prevents or delays the emergence of certain aforementioned feelings in the patient; for the therapist fails to take advantage of his potential usefulness as a role-model. (The Pedestal Syndrome again.) This furthers the denial of reality. For example, how can the patient deal with his own feelings of boredom or rage or tenderness if he senses that the therapist himself is afraid of these same feelings? In the case of the unconsciously seductive female patient, a clamp is put on the uncovering of this trait and its real motivations by a therapist who has indeed responded to her seductiveness, but who persists in denying any part in the joint emotional transaction. He sidesteps the issue with a reference to her past, thus preventing her from meeting the issue head-on. (See *It's Really Your Father:* Games.) The result is that she spends many months, plus thousands of

GAMES ANALYSTS PLAY   40

dollars, before the question of her immediate seductivity can be aired and subsequently resolved.

Unproductive games of denial on the part of the therapist prevent creative and rapid breakthroughs in the analytic process. Much truly creative and rewarding work comes about through taking advantage of the nonrational, intuitive unconscious within ourselves. Just as Freud showed that "slips of the tongue" in a patient's reportage were meaningful and useful, so can the therapist's "slips" from Standard Operating Procedure be of value to the patient. There is often a certain wisdom in the nonrational which cannot be fully appreciated until the products of that irrational spontaneity are out on the table where they can be seen and dealt with. If the therapist is uptight, overly cautious, afraid or ashamed of being unconventional in his technique—more concerned, that is, with the professional impression he is making on his patient and on his colleagues—he loses all or most of his real ability to help.

The hippies call these subtle exchanges of true feeling *vibrations*. This simply means that if X has certain feelings and attitudes toward Y, Y will, in turn, *vibrate* certain reciprocal feelings. Since these feelings are often present outside of awareness, they can be brought to the surface for examination and evaluation only if one of the parties involved is able to spot them within himself and to admit them openly. The frightened or insecure therapist cannot do this readily, and thus loses a potent tool. The patient, of course, loses even more.

The fact is that the entire psychotherapeutic profession would not be what it is today had not an intuitive man from Vienna dared to follow his instincts, in spite of the censure he received from his colleagues. Unfortunately, many of those who hold most rigorously to the theories and formulations first developed by Freud are the most hapless victims of deliberate gamesmanship, and would surely have cast the first stones at him had they been in practice fifty years ago.

PART II

Games

Games

I. GAMES TO DENY BOREDOM
   A. Diversions
   B. Tell Me a Dream
   C. Leading Question
       1. *Suppose . . . ?*
       2. *What Do You Think Would Happen If . . . ?*
       3. *How Would You Feel If . . . ?*
       4. *Have You Ever* Met *Dr. Margolis?*
       5. *What Did You Think of* Portnoy's Complaint?
       6. *Doesn't It Relate to That Affair You Had?*
   D. Describe Me as a Person

II. GAMES TO DENY IGNORANCE
    A. Oedipus
    B. Tell Me Your Feelings
    C. Opposites
    D. Tell Me Why
    E. Really? and Hhmmnn
    F. Tintoretto Has Nothing to Do with It

III. GAMES TO DENY GUILT OVER FEES
    A. Hhmmnn (replay)
    B. Stay with It
    C. I Wish You Could Hear a Tape of Yourself Three Years Ago
    D. Orthodontist
    E. Notebook

45

VIII. GAMES TO DENY THE WISH TO CONTROL
    A. My Patient
    B. I Only Asked a Question
    C. You Are Responsible for Your Own Orgasms
    D. Motivation
    E. We're Here to Analyze (or You're Acting Out)
    F. I Didn't Dream It, You Did

IX. GAMES TO DENY FEELINGS OF SUPERIORITY
    A. There Is No Difference Between Us
    B. You Don't Say!
    C. I Learn from My Patients
    D. One Day You Won't Need Me Anymore
    E. I Flunked Wood-Working 2
    F. Bathroom

X. GAMES TO DENY FEELINGS OF INFERIORITY
    A. Last Year at the Geneva Convention
    B. As Otto Rank Once Said
    C. It Sounds Like a Fugue by Bach
    D. Big Words (and Bigger Words)
    E. Diploma
    F. Twenty Questions

XI. GAMES TO DENY RIGIDITY
    A. Overtime
    B. Lateness
    C. So What?
    D. Take a Chance
    E. Four-Letter Words

XII. GAMES TO DENY LACK OF DISCIPLINE
    A. Telephone

B. Appointment Schedule
C. Notebook (replay)

XIII. GAMES PLAYED WITH SECOND-ROUNDERS
A. Hail the Conquering Hero
  1. *Dig Deeper*
  2. *You're a Victim of Countertransference*
  3. *I'll Be Frank with You*
  4. *Stop Worrying*

XIV. GAMES PLAYED WITH OTHER THERAPISTS
A. Practice-Building Games
  1. *Cocktail Party*
  2. *Lunch Hour*
  3. *Weekend Guest (Coming and Going)*
  4. *Messrs. Brooks Brothers, Abercrombie and Fitch*
  5. *My Wife*
B. Discrediting Games
  1. *Superficial*
  2. *Countertransference (replay)*
  3. *Unconventional*
C. Snare Games
  1. *Why Did You . . . ?*
  2. *Why Didn't You . . . ?*
D. Reverential Games (played with Candidates)
  1. *Let Me Tell You How I'd Have Done It*
  2. *Ask Me a Question*
  3. *So What Do You Think It Was All About?*
  4. *Mama or Papa*
  5. *Transference (replay)*
  6. *Countertransference (replay)*
E. Superannuation Games
  1. *Celebrity*

F. Podium-and-Paper Games
   1. *The Contribution of Dr. Freihoffer*
   2. *Depression as a Manifestation of Depression*
   3. *Homosexuality as Influenced by Archaic Super-Ego Introjects*
   4. *The Relationship of Eye Movements in Sleeping Fish to Castration Dreams in Six-Month-Old Males: Its Implications for Further Research in Ego Development*
   5. *The Mass-Appeal Mother-Surrogate: A Comparative Study of Gertrude Berg, Marlene Dietrich, and Carol Burnett*

XV. GAMES PLAYED SOCIALLY

A. I Have a Patient Who . . .
B. It's Your Narcissism
C. Give Me a Call and We'll See
D. Oedipal Conflict (replay)
E. Great-Grandmother
F. We
G. They
H. Ho Ho

I. Games to Deny Boredom

All people get bored from time to time. If a therapist is continually bored, he has a problem. But some therapists feel it is criminal to be bored at all. The training period has convinced them that boredom, like beauty, is in the eye of the beholder; thus, the acknowledgment of boredom is an acknowledgment of personal failure. In addition, a great number of therapists have come to regard patients as porcelain dolls who might shatter irreparably if treated to such negative evaluations. The result of these prohibitions is dishonesty. The problem is denied, and the therapist plays games:

A. Diversions

The game of *Diversions* consists of altering the mechanical aspects of treatment in order to produce some new (and, hopefully, more exciting) element in the monotonous atmosphere. The most popular diversions are based on changing the position of the patient (P). If he is using the couch, he is asked to sit up; if he is sitting up, he is asked to lie down.

It is commonly assumed that the couch itself was brought into therapeutic technique so that P, removed from the stare of the therapist (T) would be freer to fantasy and to free-associate. In truth, Freud directed his patients to the couch because *he* could not bear to be stared at for long periods of time. There are, however, other motivations which affect both T and P, either positively or negatively:

1. P who is sexually repressed is, through T's direction to

lie down, given a worthwhile test of courage. (Conversely, with the overfantasying P, the sitting-up position offers the challenge of reality.)

2. When P happens to be an attractive member of the opposite sex, her prone position, while perhaps not changing the monotonous content of her verbal productions, offers T many an enchanting hour during which to enjoy, unself-consciously, the sight of a heaving bosom or a particularly pretty pair of legs. T can, then, in all safety, resort to his own fantasy. If his feelings for P are warm and affectionate, he can string them out to fantasies of romance and possession. If his true reactions to her have, up until this point, been negative, he can engage in wishes of violence.

Other acceptable *Diversions* are:

   a. Reducing the number of P's sessions.
   b. Adding to the number of P's sessions.
   c. Raising P's fee.

B. Tell Me a Dream

Dreams have undoubtedly many values in therapy, although the countering of boredom is not among them. When used for this purpose, the playing of *Tell Me a Dream* is somewhat akin to the doing of crossword puzzles by a college freshman during zoology lectures. As the student tests his ingenuity with 45-across by turning "a common garden shrub" into "azalea"—so, with the material of a given dream, can T turn a common housewife into a reincarnated Sappho, or a despondent business executive into a brooding Prince of Denmark.

The following quiz challenges T's mastery of *Tell Me a Dream:*

Problem: P is a 28-year-old single female who works for a large corporation. She dresses conservatively, possesses a retiring nature, and has few dates. T listens to P's repetitive reports on the drabness of her life until he is too oppressed by the tedium to continue.

Choice—A or B:

A: 1. T tells P that while she is leading such an extremely colorless life, she cannot expect men to be interested in her. She must make herself more exciting. As a start, he suggests, subtly, that she affect a new hairdo, buy a miniskirt, and dab on some provocative perfume.

B: 1. T asks P to tell him a dream.
   2. P reports one in which she is in the company of an older woman who is transformed, suddenly, into a crowd of faceless men.
   3. After T has asked the proper questions and probed P's Unconscious, he helps her to reach the following insight: "It sounds terrible . . . but I guess it means I want to destroy my mother and become a prostitute . . ."
   4. P is flattered by this adventurous realization of herself and sleeps more contentedly that night.

Correct Answer: B

P's restful night, if based on the relief of this new fantasy, will wane into dawn, when once again she will have to face the reality of another bleak day. However, she will sidestep the issue of this continuing reality by reporting a new dream in her next therapeutic session.

Had T chosen A, and directed P toward new action, life could have assumed a new brightness. But the masterful player of *Tell Me a Dream* chooses B because it keeps the game going. With each new dream reported by P, T is given the opportunity to make an interesting and impressive interpretation. P, if only abstractly, will emerge as a fascinating and complicated individual whose Unconscious is as exciting as that of any world-famous courtesan. Denied: one siege of boredom.

C. Leading Question

While *Tell Me a Dream* supplies stimulation from within, *Leading Question* supplies it from without. In playing this game, T seeks (a) to get P to say something, *anything,* which will change the pace and relieve the monotony, while (b) denying that he is being directive.

Following are examples of six games of verbal exchange which form a foundation for *Leading Question:*

1. *Suppose . . . ?*
   P: (dispiritedly) I'm so tired. I had to work till 8:30 last night. My boss doesn't give a damn, he thinks I'm a machine.
   T: Suppose you told him you wouldn't work there another day?
   P: (shocked and therefore livening up) He'd have a fit! I mean, look, he's giving me a raise, and he really depends on me!
   T: Suppose you told him to drop dead? Would it kill him? Wouldn't he just hire some other sucker to do the same dirty-work?
   P: (lifting the tedium) Oh, God, I could *never!* I could just never, I simply couldn't! (Begins to tremble, perhaps to cry.)

2. *What Do You Think Would Happen If . . . ?*
   P: It's the same thing, day in, day out . . .

T: What do you think would happen if you asked your secretary to go to bed with you?

P: (brightening a bit) You know, I never thought of that.

T: How come? Didn't you once tell me she's a pretty girl?

P: Yeah. Yeah, as a matter of fact, she is . . .

T: So what's stopping you?

P: I don't know. She could maybe say no.

T: What do you think would happen if she said yes?

P thinks for a minute about what would happen. It's an
interesting thought. He begins to articulate some exciting
fantasies, and the session picks up. T is spared further dull
"day-in-day-out" comments.

3. *How Would You Feel If . . . ?*

P: I love Bill, so it doesn't matter.

T: How would you feel if you got pregnant?

P: (paling a little) Pregnant?

T: Yes. How would you feel if that happened by mistake?

P: Christ! It couldn't! We're both *married,* to other *people!*

T, who has been hearing P's love for Bill till it's coming
out of his ears, has just switched her focus onto her husband
and Bill's wife. Ergo: a change of material.

4. *Have You Ever* Met *Dr. Margolis?*

P: My friend George goes to Dr. Margolis, and he says
Margolis says dreams aren't only wishes, sometimes
they're bona fide *fears.*

T: (bored by these escapes from the real issues at hand, but
having his own emotional hangups with this colleague)
Have you ever *met* Dr. Margolis?

T removes focus from P and P's problems and gets the
chance to discuss someone who bothers him.

5. *What Did You Think of* Portnoy's Complaint?

P: I couldn't sleep. I read all night.

T: I know you read a lot.

P: I have to keep up with current stuff for the job.

T: What did you think of *Portnoy's Complaint?*

Whether T has read this particular book or not, he is aware of its subject matter. After several boring sessions with P, the intellectual lift of a book report might serve well.

6. *Doesn't It Relate to That Affair You Had?*

P: (running on, as usual, with the endless details of her life) So I went to the zoo and bought a box of cracker-jack, and then I went to the elephant place and I fed them some, but I got cold so I went into the cafeteria and got some hot chocolate and a hot dog, and then . . .

T: Doesn't it relate to that affair you had?

P, while mentally boring, can be physically interesting. Shunting her off onto the track of "that affair she had" with the social director at Camp Spookatonk the previous summer will give T a few more spates of sexual and humorous material with which to lighten his burden.

D. Describe Me as a Person

Therapists, as well as other people, are egocentric. While their professions force them to concentrate almost wholly on other people, they enjoy, immensely, being the center of attention. They can be identified with the egocentric author who says to his friend, "Now, let's talk about you. What did you think of my book?" The game of *Describe Me as a Person* can be launched successfully with the following leads:

1. Do you find me callous or sensitive?
2. If I were not your analyst, do you think you would choose me as a friend?
3. (to Ps who are artists or writers) Do you think I would make an interesting subject?

4. What kind of husband do you think I am to my wife?
5. What is your fantasy about going to bed with me?
6. Why are you afraid of me?
7. In what ways am I like your cousin Arthur?

The attractive thing about all games having to do with the denial of boredom is that T always remains unscathed, and his therapeutic technique unblemished. These games are based on suggestion. T suggests material by diverting P or asking P questions. Should the suggestion work out negatively, T is not to blame. He has only planted a few ideas, and P is responsible for all actions made upon them. It is, after all, P's own "unconscious motivations" which make him behave as he does.

While Games to Deny Boredom are negative because they are played for the sole purpose of helping T, it should also be noted that they are not the worst games in our repertory.

II. Games to Deny Ignorance

The games played most frequently by therapists are those which serve to deny ignorance—be it of cultural or historical facts, mythology, medical information, world affairs, P's own frames of reference, or the Christian name of one of 1958's winning contestants on Queen for a Day. Being human, we know only a fraction of what there is to know. Yet many therapists feel it is incumbent upon them to be all-knowing, to have all the answers, to prove to themselves and their patients that they are supremely knowledgeable. Because of this need, almost reflexively, and before he can allow his ignorance to be realized, T interrupts P's communications by either making little of them or dipping back to those constantly reiterated themes of his training.

A. Oedipus

For those T's who have been trained to accept one theme above all others, the game of *Oedipus* reigns supreme. Freud's special relationship with his mother led him to believe that all young boys wish to eliminate their fathers and marry their mothers. As the world's first psychoanalyst, he had enormous advantages. He was the first in print; he could readily demonstrate the Oedipal Conflict in all his students and patients (those who failed to see it were deemed to be "resisting"), and he had a large number of students who spread the word in geometric progression.

In actuality, *Oedipus* is a simple game that involves the translation of all human responses and relationships into a

57

symbology which neatly matches Freud's original thesis. The mind boggles at the thought of what the therapeutic scene would be today had Camille been the world's first analyst and *The Trojan Women* her theme.

P: Today, when I was coming here, I dropped my umbrella.
T: How did that happen?
P: I had this big package to carry, and it was too much.
T: Very Oedipal . . .

By the time the session is over, T has successfully directed P to the insight that the umbrella, a phallic symbol, was really his father, whom he wished, as a child, to "drop," or "get rid of"; that the package, being a container of something, was in truth the womb; and that the desire on P's part to "carry" this womb and not "drop it" proves his neurotic attachment to his mother. Since it is difficult to explain why any person in the rain, loaded with umbrella and large parcel, and rushing toward a destination might *not* experience some trouble, it is best to play a quick round of Oedipus in order to get the problem out of the way. Yet T has, by purely analytic standards, been impressive.

B.   Tell Me Your Feelings

Therapists interested in altering patient-behavior must know much about P's activities; they must locate those interactions which might be amenable to change. Behavioral therapists are more concerned with what the patient does, whom he does it with, and what the other person does in return.

Nonbehavioral therapists are apt to forget or overlook the importance of activity and to lapse into the role of pseudophilosopher or emotional historian, devoting unnecessary time to the study of feelings and their place in the life of man. Regardless of what patients bring to their therapeutic sessions, the antiaction therapist, feeling safe in the rut of his classical training, invariably directs the discussion to one of emotional reaction.

Tell Me Your Feelings is a game which can turn P into a lyric poet or an insufferable bore; for P learns early that it is not simply what he feels that counts, but, importantly, the exquisiteness with which he can describe it.

Tell Me Your Feelings is a harmless enough game in that it will not make P any worse; but aside from the creation of more moving articulations of his problems, it will not make him any better.

The material obtained by nonbehavioral therapists differs vastly from that obtained by behavioral therapists.

Following are three illustrations of that difference:

1. A 17-year-old boy reports that his girl has stood him up.
   a. The *Tell Me Your Feelings* therapist discovers that P is experiencing sadness and anger.
   b. The action-oriented therapist discovers that P has been dating a 54-year-old woman.
2. A 26-year-old woman reports that she has lost her job.
   a. The *Tell Me Your Feelings* therapist discovers that P is burdened by a sense of failure, of worthlessness.
   b. The action-oriented therapist discovers that P, upon being asked to do some extra work at time-and-a-half overtime, told her boss to "jerk off."
3. A 42-year-old man reports that he hasn't had a date in seven years.
   a. The *Tell Me Your Feelings* therapist discovers that P is beset by loneliness.
   b. The action-oriented therapist discovers that, except for meals and doctors' appointments, P has not left his mother's apartment for seven years.

Players of *Tell Me Your Feelings* are able to avoid head-on collisions with reality-situations, and to hide ignorance of solutions interminably by sticking with the discovery and analysis of emotional phenomena.

C. Opposites

So built into the therapist is the concept of Opposites that it can be considered a rote game. While it is played automatically and without clear purpose in mind (as are other ignorance games), its effect is to confuse P badly. For P soon begins to wonder if he can ever take anything he himself does at face value.

One requirement for the playing of *Opposite*s is T's development of an attitude of suspicion and an ability to transmit this suspicion to P. T must see hidden meanings everywhere and be especially sensitive to reaction-formations. A reaction-formation involves a process by which a socially acceptable reaction exaggerates itself to mask a less noble motivation. The classic example is the man who becomes a surgeon and saves life, thereby covering, and partially gratifying, a sadistic tendency to mutilate.

The director of psychiatric training at a well-known metropolitan hospital, himself a nationally acclaimed analyst, once addressed his resident group as follows:

"When a patient tells you about a dream in which a log floats down a body of water, you'd do well to think about birth-trauma. If he tells you about birth-trauma, you ought to find out if he's had some recent experiences with water."

This man was a past-master at the game of *Opposites*. Yet considering the training ground T has traveled, it can be seen that very little additional gardening is needed to cultivate this therapeutically perverse attitude.

Here are verbal exchanges which illustrate the game in action:

(1) P: I really love my wife.

    T: It seems to me that you are trying to hide the fact that you hate her.

(2) P: My mother was terrible and I hated her.

    T: Perhaps what you are really trying to tell me is that you loved her too much.

(3) P: I feel extremely generous today. I just donated $5,000 to the Allied Jewish Appeal.

    T: Mightn't you have done this because you wanted to give Jews something to make up for the love you weren't given in childhood? If so, this would mean, of course, that you gave not so much out of generosity, but out of a wish to get something.

D. Tell Me Why

While *Opposites* is not meant, consciously, to confuse, *Tell Me Why* is played for precisely that purpose. This derives from a popular game played by elementary school teachers who, when confronted with the absence of homework, ask the child, "Why didn't you do it?" Children, being more imaginative than adults (and more vulnerable, too), usually try to help out the teacher and themselves by providing an answer—any answer:

    a. "My dog was sick."

    b. "My eyes hurt."

    c. "We had to go to my grandmother's funeral."

    d. "My sister stole the electric bulb."

Unfortunately, the child who goes along with *Tell Me Why* is worse off than the one who answers, "I don't know." For what the teacher seeks is an excuse so flimsy that she can publicly humiliate the child who has failed her. In truth, few of us know why we do, or do not do, certain things, other than the fact that we "felt like it." But we can always provide some sort of rationalization, should anyone demand it of us. We can, though, report with reasonable accuracy what we did "instead of"—or what we did "after."

Yet the *Tell Me Why* therapist is not interested in the facts. He is concerned with proving that he is one step ahead of the patient. He can hide his ignorance of life-solutions by relying on a long analysis of Why, rather than launching into *What* and *What-to-do-about-it*.

Here is *Tell Me Why,* played by a diligent T and an equally stubborn and recalcitrant P:

> T: Tell me why you saw Paula last night.
> P: Oh, I don't know. Just decided to, I guess.
> T: Just decided?
> P: Well, Paula's okay. Why not Paula?
> T: The question is *why* Paula.
> P: I really don't know.
> T: Think about it for a minute. It could be important . . .

With each suggestion from T that P "think about it," P grows more apprehensive about the importance of an unanswered question which may change his entire therapeutic history. The game can continue endlessly:

> P: (finally giving in) She reminds me of a girl I knew at college—a girl I sat next to in Advanced Calculus.
> T: Tell me why you studied Advanced Calculus.

E.   Really? and Hhmmnn

There are no other games in the therapeutic lexicon as patently absurd, yet as sharply effective, as *Really?* and *Hhmmnn*. Ignorance of all kinds can be sidestepped by the use of either of them.

> P: I had a really great dream last night. I was in the Louvre, standing in front of this painting by Tintoretto.
> R: Really?

P: The painting came alive for me. In each color, in each area of spacial development, I could see something which related to the things I've been telling you about for a month.

T: Hhmmnn.

F. Tintoretto Has Nothing to Do with It

This game is, obviously, an extended version of *Really?* and *Hhmmnn*. If *Really?* and *Hhmmnn* are not sufficient to make T feel at ease with the denial of his ignorance, he can become more aggressive and eliminate the troubling issue entirely. P in this case is, after all, a rather intelligent and complex human being. It is quite possible that he will recognize T's evasions for what they are. He will sense, empathically, that these one-word and one-sound responses mean an absence of real knowledge on T's part. Hence, when P says, "I was in the Louvre, standing in front of this painting by Tintoretto"—T can stop P's esoteric frame of reference entirely by interrupting with: "Tintoretto has nothing to do with it."

Similarly, a P in treatment with an unaware T, once presented a dream which related, in quality, to a short story by Truman Capote. When told that "Truman Capote had nothing to do with it," P, unfazed, asked, "Have you ever read Truman Capote?" T's answer to this was, "I don't have to read about things; I experience them firsthand." To which P, still unfazed, asked, "How did you do as a soldier in the Peloponnesian Wars?" Several months later P was terminated on the grounds that she was "too resistant to the therapy."

III.   Games to Deny Guilt over Fees

Given the normal amount of egocentricity in all Ts, a task
which basically consists in listening to other people talk
about themselves is no easy chunk to swallow. On the other
hand, it is an exciting business. Also, there are many times
when people prefer to listen, to keep the focus on someone
else who will save them the malaise of exposing themselves.
There are times, too, when Ts are highly stimulated by
visible progress, or by P's articulated material itself. Ts learn
much from patients which they are then able to use in their
own lives. They are respected and needed. They are important. To be paid so well in addition often leads to guilt-
feelings—particularly at those times when there is nothing
for them to do *except* listen. It is then that they feel impelled
to throw in a little something extra to justify their recompen-
sation. Games to deny guilt over fees are relatively harmless.
Nonetheless, they are worth noting:

A.   Hhmmnn (replay)

Hhmmnn is a game which crops up continuously throughout the course of therapy, but the motivations differ. While
we have just shown it to be a game to deny ignorance, it is
also a game which proves that we are actually there and
working. Variations on *Hhmmnn* are *Uh-huh, Um, Yes . . .,
Ah . . .*, and *Well. . . .* When all else fails, a good, healthy
clearing of the throat will serve the same purpose.

Hhmmnn and its substitutes play their guilt-salving part in
several ways:

64

a. They allow P to hear the sound of T's voice.
b. They allow T to hear the sound of his own voice.
c. They provide T with a feeling of usefulness.
d. They provide T with an outlet for stored-up nervous energy.
e. They make T sound noncommittal and therefore extremely professional, particularly in the case of psychoanalysts.

When P hears *Hhmmnn* he knows for certain that he is in therapy and getting something for his money.

B.   Stay with It

It is enormously difficult to admit defeat. Although many therapists have referred patients to other therapists, the switch, for whatever good reason it might have been made, bears the ring of failure. Always, a patient who is suddenly terminated, or directed to other sources of help, leaves with the feeling that he has wasted time, energy, and money. And the therapist whom he leaves wonders, guiltily, if he has been worth his fees.

Classical analysis has been known to continue with one P and one T for years. Even at the very last ditch, when P's ego or self-esteem has been healed to the point where he is able to see that a change might be in order, he is told by T, "Stay with it." More often than not, he does. For one thing, he feels that a known evil is better than an unknown good; for another, T has demonstrated his own stick-to-it-iveness, his own assiduousness and diligence as a professional, and whether "staying with it" is objectively valid or not, he seems worth the expenditure of a further chance.

Those who have not undergone deep analysis wonder how patients do make the final break from therapy. Terminations arise from any of a number of situations, some good, others harmful:

1. The moving of T to another city or state while P is still in a developmental stage. Rather than face the challenge of having to "do it all over again" with a new T, P may decide to chance things on his own—before he is ready.
2. The death of T which brings with it such real trauma for P, and, in analytic terms, spells such irrevocable "rejection" of him by T, that he may flounder for as long as a year or more before seeking other help.
3. The refusal of an insecure T to go on with the course of therapy owing to what he feels to be an unbreakable resistance or negative transference on P's part.
4. The Honorable Discharge:
   The honorable discharge from therapy comes only as a result of P's accumulative health. It is manifested by P's verbal productions. While once he spoke needfully of his life-and-death dependence on T, he now begins to say instead:
   a. When you went on your vacation, it wasn't half bad. I got used to not coming to sessions. I really *liked* living without you, making my own decisions, and all. It felt good. To tell you the truth, I'm sort of sorry you came back.
   b. I've heard you say those same things over and over again. It's not just in my head; my life is changing, too. I get the feeling maybe you've given me all you have to give.
   c. I dreamed last night I was in a station, about to board a train. I think you were in the station somewhere, even though it didn't look exactly like you. I knew I was going to board the train in a minute or two, so I looked for you—because I wanted to say good-bye.

    d. I dreamed you died, and I was at the funeral. But it wasn't sad. It was sort of a party. I didn't cry. I was having a good time.

    e. I dreamed I was standing on a street corner with a police dog. We were waiting for a bus. Two buses came up together. I got into one, and the dog got into another, and then we were going in opposite directions. I waved at him. I said, "So long, Fido, old boy," but suddenly he wasn't a dog, he was you!

These productions expose P's fantasies of leaving T. They well up from his unconscious mind as signals to inform himself consciously that he is getting ready to go free. The wish, however, does not become a *fait accompli* for quite some time, particularly if his T is a *Stay with It* player. The Leaving Fantasy will continue for months, with many verbal repetitions. T will suggest that P "work through" the fantasies so that he can better understand his motivations: are they good wishes, or are they unreal cover-ups for the desire to escape further work?

The P who has the courage to say, "I'm finished!" who indeed terminates his own therapy, is often so guilt-laden by T's disapproval that he will be back again within a week.

The time to leave is a question of delicate mechanisms operating within both P and T. When the traditional T labels P's decision "acting out," P may go, but not freely. The behavioral T will be more open to P's wish to leave, and he will welcome P's chance to try living without help.

In classical therapy, *Stay with It* is often a manifestation of T's own feelings of rejection, of having failed, or of not being worthwhile.

C. I Wish You Could Hear a Tape of Yourself Three Years Ago

This game is in fact a more subtle version of *Stay with It*. P, after innumerable sessions, comes to the end of a particu-

larly fruitless hour. As he is ready to leave T's office, he turns
in his tracks and fixes T with a depressed stare.

T: Hhmmnn?
P: I feel awful.
T: Um . . . why?
P: Well, it seems like we're just not getting anywhere.
T: How so?
P: How much longer am I going to lie there telling you my
   mother was an obsessional neurotic with neatness
   rituals? We know already how I suffered from the starch
   in my diapers. I just don't think we're making progress.
T: (with a kind, fatherly, and condescending smile) Not
   making progress? I wish you could hear a tape of your-
   self three years ago.

D. Orthodontist

T has been working hard with P, collecting, for each hour,
a sum of money which has P's budget down to the point
where he is out of shoes and wearing his sister's bedroom
slippers. This situation is adding to P's already sizable store
of emotional problems, and he asks T if he might have an
extra hour, say on Saturday morning. T is also aware of the
situation, becomes victimized by guilt, and attempts to salve
his conscience. If he is worthy in any sense at all of his
responsibility as a therapist, he is above telling lies, or
manufacturing situations; but he, like any other human
being, is apt to use a true set of circumstances to best advantage. He says, "I'm afraid I can't on Saturday. I have to take
my little girl to the orthodontist." The guilt has been switched.
P leaves with the knowledge that T has as many expenses to
meet as *he* has—if not more—and T feels vindicated.

Orthodontist has many variations. The following are only a
few:

(a) I'm visiting my older son at the leprosy colony.

(b) I'm moving my widowed mother-in-law into the house.

(c) I promised my wife I'd go shopping to buy her a new oxygen tent.

E. Notebook

There is no verbal exchange in the game of Notebook. It is a gestural game, which can be played at any time, for the purpose of proving busy-ness and a serious attitude toward P's productions. Many Ts in the psychoanalytic category keep a separate notebook for each P, into which are written, as P utters them, important dream sequences, free associations, and so on. Depending upon the degree of legibility, T can, if he wishes, refer back to these notes before P arrives so that he will not be too surprised by material which seems new when in fact it has been articulated at the previous session.

Pencils and ballpoint pens are practically noiseless. It is best if T uses a thin-line fountain pen which scratches. The sound may disconcert P if he is a beginner, but in due course he will adjust to this annoyance, even come to depend on it unconsciously, as one might to the familiar ticking of a clock or spring rain at night on a windowpane.

P: (on couch, facing away from T) What're you *doing* back there?

T: (softly, solicitously) I'm writing down the things you are saying . . .

There is little doubt that T is working. He is on the job and earning his pay.

F. I'm Not in It for the Money

P: (male) You don't really care about me.

T: (female) Yes, I do.

P: Nah, you don't. If I died tomorrow you'd just get someone else to give you the dough.

T: There's more to it than that.

P: I come here to get love, and I pay for it. I could just as
well go to a whorehouse!

T: I care very much about you. I care about helping you.
I'm not in it for the money . . .

P, as we already know, is a person beset by grave insecuri-
ties. He is also hypersensitive. The combination of these two
traits leads to a degree of paranoia. He feels that he is being
used unfairly, exploited, duped. As his self-confidence builds,
he is able to voice these fantasies. T, also human, has his own
doubts. As P continues to question T's value and his motivations, T becomes defensive.

G.   If You Didn't Pay You'd Feel Guilty

This same P continues to doubt T's motivations and to
make T defensive about them:

P: If you weren't in it for the money, you wouldn't charge
so much.

T: On your birthday didn't I give you a free hour? Don't
you remember that?

P: It wasn't my birthday. It was Christmas week.

T: All right, same thing.

P: Still, you wouldn't charge so much.

T: Look now, be reasonable. We are two adults doing
work in which there is an exchange of values. I am
giving you something important. *If you didn't pay,
you'd feel guilty.*

Now both T and P are on the defensive. P, in his morass
of self-doubt, needs, more than likely, to learn to take as well
as to give; he must learn to feel *worthy* of taking. His

production, in this case, is a healthy indication of his wish to feel worthy; yet he is stymied by T's subtle admonition. *If you didn't pay, you'd feel guilty* might be replaced with better results if T were honest enough to say: *Since I give to you, I wish to be rewarded.* In this way he (she) becomes a role-model for P, who will also feel, in time, that he is deserving of a return in life for his efforts.

IV. Games to Deny Hostility

Among people of Western culture, anger is the most difficult emotion to handle. For that reason, games played in this area are the most potentially destructive. For how can T help P to realize this emotion if T is unable to realize it within himself? Few, if any of us, ever come to a complete resolution of this problem. Our mores dictate that we suppress hostility for the sake of civilization. Yet the savage within us (which Freud called the Id) continues to survive in spite of all discouragement. And when too much suppression is applied, what may have been a simple and harmless anger grows, expands, and often bursts through with greater violence.

Games played by therapists to deny hostility serve to further bottle the emotion. Thus, each ploy used against the patient, indirectly, subtly, multiplies, and in fact carries with it a quality of cruelty.

A. Castrator!

Castrator! is a favorite form of hostility-denial among male Ts when dealing with female Ps. Indeed, it is a favorite form of hostility-denial among most American males dealing with females, and Ts can hardly be expected to be exempt. The game can be called nothing less than lethal, because it plays upon the female's most extreme fear. If she were, in truth, a castrator, she would rid the world of all the males on whom she so deeply depends, and whom she needs desperately in order to establish her womanhood. Poetic and amorous Sappho, on her island of females, was on one level a figure of

72

high romance. On another level, she was an escapist and a feminine failure.

The role of Lesbian has its special charm. There are few women who have not at some time, in or out of awareness, consciously or unconsciously, toyed with the fantasy of retreat from the battle of the sexes in order to settle into the tender nest of female consortion. For homosexuality is, in reality, a form of narcissism: one gazes into the complex pool of love only to find the comforting reflection of self.

Yet, in our society, this choice has been deluged with taboos, both psychological and legalistic. There is, therefore, no better way to strike dread into the heart of a woman than by subtly suggesting her tendency to castrate. To castrate is, literally, to deprive men of their sexual organs; figuratively, to weaken them or to kill them psychologically. The female castrator, then, is left to the devices of other women.

Take T, at the height of frustration in the course of therapy with a difficult female P: He has learned in his training that any real show of anger proves him to be neurotic. At all costs to himself, he must retain neutrality. Where is his anger to go? He cannot tell P to "go shove it" or to stop bugging him. He must, instead, play a game.

P: (sensing T's rising anger, and pleased with her success at driving him to a human response) So I keep forgetting my hours, so what? Don't *you* ever forget anything? Anyhow, I was spending the day with Peter, and you can just bet your ass I'm not going to think about you when I'm with Peter.

T: Your hours come before anything else, you know that.

P: Yes? Well, some days they don't.

T: (swallowing his resentment) I can't do you much good if you . . . render me helpless.

P: (sensing the implication unconsciously and trying to backtrack) Oh, go to hell. I mean, listen . . .

T: You're very hostile today, aren't you?

P: Yes, I am.

T: You are hostile to men in general, aren't you? Even to Peter at times?

P: At times, yes. I suppose so . . . when he's impossible.

T: What do you suppose your motivation might be in trying to hurt men? What do you find so impossible about them?

P: Oh, I don't know.

T: Perhaps their sexuality? Is that what you'd like to take away from them?

P: (remains silent)

In effect, T has shouted the word *Castrator!* at P, and she has no weapons left with which to fight. There is little for her to do but spend the ensuing year or so delving into her psyche for the causes of her castration tendencies. During that period of time she will lose sight of herself as a "real woman," which, in fact, she is. Actually, her display of anger at T was a healthy sign of self-assertion. But it has now been squelched. T has hit her where it really hurts. His own hostility has been hidden behind the irrefutable defense of a psychiatric implication.

Substitutes for Castrator! are:

1. Frigid!
2. Manipulator!
3. Ball-breaker!
4. Bitch Goddess!
5. Masculine Woman!

Of the five, Masculine Woman! is the most effective. Freud himself, when faced with a particularly brilliant and self-assertive female P, remarked that she was not really a woman, but more like a man.

The game is a dangerous one. For there is nothing so well calculated to turn a woman into an aggressive battle-ax as suggesting to her that she is masculine.

B. Confrontation

People in treatment are often totally unaware of the impression they make on others. Because of this, the confrontation of P by T is, at certain points, an essential part of the therapeutic process. Basically, such confrontation should enable P to see his assets as well as his liabilities. Indeed, many Ps miss the boat in that they are certain that others view them negatively when in truth they are well received.

The game of Confrontation, in the variation considered, is a form which is employed by the angry T as a ploy to deny his hostility. He concentrates his attack on the patient, thus relieving his own irritation, and, at the time, stays within the limits of safety by keeping his criticism within the acceptable therapeutic framework.

The T who plays *Confrontation* invariably prides himself on his ability to talk openly, fast, and to the point. He conveys in the minimal number of words the maximal amount of ego-smashing material. His slogan is, "What your best friends won't tell you, I will." And what he tells is indeed difficult for any P to accept with equanimity. To the *Confrontation* player, such things as tact and subtlety are irrelevant if not downright equivocative. T's motivation here, we must remember, is negative. Were he to play the game for the positive purpose of enlightening P, the results would prove more valid. But when he uses it as a hostility denial, the punches are wild, pulled in from left field. So far as timing is concerned, T chooses his own moment of need, disregarding P's state of mind.

A few *Confrontation* gambits are:

a. Your husband wants a woman; you're still a little girl.
b. If you drink before you come to your next session, I will terminate your therapy.
c. Face it—you're a nymphomaniac.
d. If you don't screw your wife regularly, you can't expect her to be faithful.
e. You think you're great? That's just the residual element of your *infant-autism*.

While these admonitions might be helpful to P in certain circumstances, they are, in the case of the Confrontation player, merely outlets for denied hostility; they either glance off or cause setbacks in P's progress toward self-confidence.

C. Switchies

Switchies is a clever game used by T to *prevent* the mounting of hostility within himself. It is played by taking anything P says and turning it right back on him:

1. *I'd Like to Ask You*
   P: (male) You look like a cow.
   T: (female) I'd like to ask you . . . what's your preoccupation with cows all about?

2. *This Is Your Analysis, Not Mine*
   P: It occurs to me that you keep patients waiting anywhere from five minutes to half an hour. Whatever patient you have in here, you run overtime. What happened in *your* childhood that makes you late all the time?
   T: Come now, don't forget this is *your* analysis, not mine.

3. *Why Did You Ask Me That Question?*

    P: If cigars are phallic symbols, how come you've always got one stuck into your mouth?

    T: Why did you ask me that question?

4. *What It Really Is, Is . . .*

    P: What you said about my being a latent homosexual doesn't click right with me. I mean, I used to whittle sticks when I was a boy. After all, I was creating things out of the stick. I was carving it into a little boat-mast or an arrow. So I think your interpretation is pretty wrong.

    T: What it really is, is your own penis that you were cutting down.

As T continues to prevent his anger from showing, P loses the chance to see it in action, which results in his being afraid to show his own.

5. *That's* Your *Problem*

This variation on *Switchies* is the most destructive of all. It is a game which has become popular in many relationships, including those outside of therapy. In therapy, it brings with it a discouragement which acts against P's future freedom to ask for help. Say P has been unavoidably detained from his hour. He rushes in to find T has already started with his next P, who has come early. T, already hostile because his schedule has been disordered, is in no mood to accept "excuses." P, on the other hand, is genuinely sorry, upset, and desirous of expressing himself in order to clear away his guilt.

    P: Honestly, I couldn't help it. And if I wait for this patient to get through, I'll be late getting back to the office. There's a meeting today, and I just can't take off two hours.

T: That's *your* problem. If you like, we'll discuss it tomorrow, at your regular time.

P, who has done nothing wrong, is filled with guilt by T's
superior denial of anger—which would rightly be directed at
himself. T has, after all, given P's time to another patient.

V. Games to Deny Loss of Contact

Interpersonal losses of contact are par for the human course. Often we say to ourselves, "My mind went blank"—or, "I guess I just drifted off into space." Games to deny boredom have some similarity to games which deny loss of contact. Their difference lies in the fact that boredom is an active response to something, a condition of irritation, while loss of contact is the cessation of response altogether.

The laymen takes loss of contact in himself pretty much for granted. Therapists, however, believe that drift-offs are indicative of failure and therefore try to hide them. Most therapists dread being caught napping, actually sleeping, by their patients; although, in fact, some have been caught doing so on occasion.

The following games are devised to minimize that risk:

A. The Silent Treatment

T is trained to sit quietly and attentively while P talks, the purpose being to allow P ample time to probe his own psyche through the processes of free association and reportage of dreams and wakeful incidents. Silence, however, becomes a game when T uses it to deny the fact that he has drifted off. It is difficult for P to know whether T's silence is employed to aid P, or whether it is a contrivance to aid T himself, for it would take a very exceptional T to admit the latter. The difficulty is compounded when P uses the couch and cannot get a good look at T during T's silences. Snoring would, of course, expose T in spite of P's position, but such an exaggerated degree of drift-off is rare.

If P has reached an ego-point where he is able to make demands on T, he can test T's silence by asking to be allowed to sit up. But T, mindful of the game, would then suggest that P remain prone for the sake of better fantasy productions.

B.   Say That Again

Freud discovered that when patients retold their dreams they frequently included material in the second telling which had been missing from the first. The same phenomenon occurs in the recounting of wakeful experiences. Thus, it is entirely appropriate for T to ask P to repeat what he has already said. *Say That Again,* when it is played merely for the purpose of masking T's inattentiveness, can be more convincing if he concentrates on the style in which the phrase is uttered. Best results are obtained, particularly when P is already sitting up, if T:

a. hunches forward
b. wrings his hands
c. wrinkles his brow, puffs intently on his pipe, cigar or cigarette
d. encourages a new spate of material by using his please-pay-careful-attention voice.

This last device works on two scores: P is given a small shot of T's authority; and T is, in actuality, reminding himself that attention must be paid.

The T who has chronic difficulty in attending to what his Ps are saying is in an extremely distressing position. He is left wide open to a game initiated by P, called *Unpaid Bill.*

C.   That Reminds Me

While T has been trained to speak of himself and of his other Ps as little as possible, there is nothing like self-focus to snap him to attention. Conscious of his loss of contact, hearing P's voice as a meaningless drone in the distance, he can re-amass his artillery by cutting in with, *That Reminds Me* . . .

    a. of an interesting discovery I made at my training center;
    b. of a patient I had several years ago;
    c. of a book you might like to read when your therapy terminates;
    d. of an argument my cook had with the butler next door.

It is of little importance whether the recollection actually relates to what P has been saying. P already realizes that all thought-productions have vital relationships in the Unconscious.

VI.   Games to Deny Sexual Interest

If T is a "well person," he is going to respond sexually to various types of female Ps. He has been trained, however, to view such responses as an indication of countertransference—the most dreaded of all therapeutic pitfalls. For this reason, he denies his reactions by dressing them in the respectable armor of Technique. In fact, this device is not so much a denial of actual response as, rather, a safe method for receiving gratification without obviously "acting out" on his true impulses:

A.   Lie Down, I Want to Talk to You

Lie Down, I Want to Talk to You is titled thusly in recollection of the punchline of an old joke about a man who has decided to treat his date to a little intellectual consideration. In T's case, the game-prop is the couch. If P happens to be a budding starlet whose therapy has been currently involved with sitting up in order to face reality, T can safely switch techniques. He can, in complete unawareness of motivation, decide, suddenly, that she would fare better with free association by lying down.

B.   Transference

Transference is an insidious, if hilarious, game. For our purposes we will use the male T and the female P.

T, either consciously or unconsciously smitten by P, is plunged into the depths of despair and frustration by P's apparent lack of sexual interest in him. He has on hand a device which is foolproof because it is based on one of the principal theories of psychoanalysis: In order to dredge up and study the past, P uses T as a surrogate, or substitute object, for all the feelings (and actions) of incest, sexual desire, aggressivity, rejection, love, hate (which is love denied), and perversions which troubled her in childhood. In effect, P must *transfer* these emotions to T whole-hog if therapy is to end with any measure of success. The P who is unable to *transfer* is unable to relive the past, and therefore unable to grasp its true meanings, as applied to the present.

P, in the following verbal exchange, has actually been loath to make the transference because she realizes, unconsciously, that an avalanche of material relating to her father, brothers, or erstwhile boyfriends, if replaced and focused on T, will lead to a painful involvement with him. To "fall in love" with a "transference-therapist" is about as pleasurable and rewarding as falling in love with an impotent giraffe. For T, once he realizes that such a transference has been made to him, becomes totally professional and unresponsive.

The following T, however, has not yet realized that such a complication is in the offing. He senses only that he is being rejected. So he plays the following game:

P: I dreamed I was walking down an empty street in a strange city. Suddenly I saw this fountain pen, or pencil, or something like that, lying on the sidewalk. Somehow it struck me as being valuable, so I picked it up . . .

T: What did you do with it?

P: I took it with me.

T: How?

P: What do you mean?

T: How did you take it with you?

P: I just . . . well, I had it in my hand, and then, I just took it with me.

T: Did you keep it in your hand?

P: (blushing) No.

T: Where did you put it?

P: In my . . . pants.

T: You were wearing pants?

P: I mean my underwear, my panties.

T: Ah. And why did you do *that?*

P: I didn't have any pockets.

T: Is that the real reason?

P: (beginning to perspire) Well . . . no. I had the feeling . . . in the dream, I mean . . . that it would feel good in there.

T: In where?

P: In my panties.

T: Come now, you're not being entirely honest with me, are you? You know the rules of therapy. You must tell me your dreams accurately. You must tell me everything that comes to your mind. It is against the rules to suppress.

P: All right! I . . . I inserted it.

T: Inserted it where?

P: You *know* where!

T: Say the word.

P: Va . . . Vagina!

T: Good. Now free-associate.

P: What?

T: Free-associate. What does the fountain pen, or the pencil, remind you of?

P: (angrily) Lissen, I know all that crap already. So it's really a prick. So *okay!*

T: And whose "prick" is it, do you suppose?

P: (quickly) My boyfriend Marvin's.

T: You're sure?

P: Well, for God's sake, whose else could it be?

T: Mine perhaps?

P: That is utterly fantastic!

T: Fantasy, yes. Fantastic, no.

P: Why would I dream a thing like that about *you*, for God's sake?

T: *Transference* . . .

The seed has been planted by T in P's Unconscious. The chances are ten to one that, in the ensuing days or weeks, P will have, and report, a dream which involves sexual relations with T. Marvin will be forgotten for the time being, and T will enjoy P's transference until it falls upon him to quench the flame by informing her that it is really her brother Erwin's.

Games which are played on the same lines as *Transference* are:

1. Repression
2. Resistance

Whatever P's verbal productions may be, T can always force the desired result by suggesting that P is *repressing* the true story, or *resisting* him.

C. Beautiful Wife

If T's sexual countertransference becomes too hot to handle, he himself can replace his feelings onto another object, such as his wife. P, he knows, will be amenable to any and all discussions involving T's personal life. It will take very little for T to direct P into sexual questions. Beautiful Wife is an unfair game. In effect, P, all unawares, is being used by T as an agent in getting him to stay married.

VII. Games to Deny Love

Games to deny love are sad games. There is nothing funny about them at all. They are the dismal indication of what our frightened and self-conscious society has become. Freud himself could not have known that his admonition against countertransference would lead to a structured denial of the most productive of all human emotions.

In these games there are no winners; there are only losers. It is a joy and a rarity to give and to receive affection, and both T and P are the poorer when such genuine feelings are forced into denial. Ironically, the display of real love-emotion is a fine tool which T might use to build trust into P's impoverished psyche, and such trust and caring would serve to expand P's limited range of productions. P is, as has already been stated, lacking in self-esteem, subject to fear and the expectation of eternal rejection. In many cases, it takes years before P dares to free associate, dares even to expose his conscious thoughts and feelings. For T is often viewed as the Enemy, to be revered and feared at the same time.

T, himself uncertain of his role, suddenly aware of his warm reactions, retreats from them like a panicked pismire, and plays games:

A. Professional

Professional is, of course, the Game of Games. Its concept is present in each and every therapeutic game, in each and every variation. What T does in private life is, more or less, his own affair—yet even here he tends to put his professional foot forward. (See *Games Therapists Play Socially.*) It is no small thing to T that he is a member of the Professional Class; neither his training nor his own rigidity will allow him to forget it for long. People come and people go, but it is essential, even years after termination, to think of them as Patients. Once upon a time there was a unique T whose affection got the better of her. "I don't want to be your psychiatrist," she told her patient, "I want to be your friend." It was during the course of the friendship that T and her ex-P made many intellectual and emotional exchanges. There was no further need for P to search for help elsewhere. But such incidents are rare.

B. No Apples

Marguerite Sechehaye, a female European psychologist, developed the concept of Symbolic Realization. She took into her home a young female schizophrenic whom she treated for many hours each day. When the girl, sitting in Sechehaye's lap, wanted to fondle her breasts, Sechehaye gave her apples instead. The apples were a symbol of love, yet they were real, and helped the child to circumvent a homosexual transference.

American disciples of Freud do not believe in the exchange of gifts. Their theory is that such a transaction causes guilt on both sides. Actually, No Apples, or it's equivalent, is a gamey attitude which serves to deny guilt over the impulse to show love.

C. I Have Other Patients

The residuals of infant autism in all of us tend to persist in our adulthoods, and to prompt us to demand, particularly in relationships which are fraught with admiration and unattainable desires, that we be the most important of all objects to those whom we love or need. The normal infant knows and cares only about himself. He is the focal object of his parents' love and attention; he is conscious only of the small world of his crib or playpen, and fully expects, without thought or reason, to be fed, bathed, dressed, and protected. When this expectation is carried forth into adulthood, it causes neurosis, to say nothing of pain and disappointment, since it is impossible to receive *total* consideration from any other single human being.

In spite of an awareness of this impossibility, the therapeutic patient has a stubborn and unrelenting fantasy: "I am really his (or her) Favorite Patient. Nobody deserves as much interest and care as I do. It is essential that I be loved and held above all others."

Often, a therapist responds—either to this fantasy, or to feelings of love and affection within himself, for a particular patient. Yet his training has dictated that favoritism be denied.

There comes a time in the course of deep therapy when P is able to voice these demands openly and without shame. Emotionality is no longer so guarded as it was; weeping, pleading, writhing with wantfulness can be indulged in as a means of swaying T to agreement.

Since one of the greatest achievements for any T is to bring P to the point of such unabashed honesty, it is, in many cases, detrimental to both P and the progress of therapy to discourage these genuine outbursts of feeling. However, T, bound by certain set rules, and his fear of countertransference, shies away.

P: Tell me, tell me! I am your best patient, aren't I? I'm interesting! I bring you good material! I cooperate. I even made you laugh out loud a few months ago! You think of me a lot, don't you? You'd rather have me here than somebody else?

T: (trying for kindliness, but bursting the balloon) Well, you know, don't you, that *I have other patients* . . .

Since Ts of all classes are essentially father or mother surrogates, the competition P feels with other Ps is very much akin to sibling rivalry. The good parent, when faced with the emotional demands of several children, sees to it that each one is praised, is made to feel precious and cherished for his own unique qualities. When the child says, "Mommy, do you love me?" the sensitive and constructive mother does not answer, "Well, you know, don't you, that I have other children . . ."

I Have Other Patients is often a devastating and harmful game. T gets himself off the hook quite neatly; but P must spend much subsequent time in recovering security which has already been gained, only to be lost again.

D. It's Really Your Father

P: (sincerely) I really like you. I mean, not just because you're trying to help me. I like you as a person. You're the kind of guy I'd like to know and pal around with. You look right. You've got a sense of humor. And I like the way you do things.

T: (retreating emotionally) Well, now, that's nice. But it's not me you're having these feelings about. *It's really your father* . . .

In this illustration, P is a young male patient who has developed real fondness for his male T. T, actually reciprocating the emotion, but wary of it, directs P to the realization that the object of affection and admiration has been misplaced through the inner processes of transference.

E. Placation

*Placati*on is an extension of *It's Really Your Father.*
Repeat P: I like you as a person. You're the kind of guy I'd like to know and pal around with. You've got a sense of humor, etc., etc.
T: You don't need to butter me up. That's placation . . .

F. I Love the Little Girl in You

P was, once, long ago, an unloved child. Her father was a salesman who traveled extensively, leaving her with her mother for long periods of time. Now P is an adult. Granted, her present-day attitudes have basis in past paternal rejection. On the other hand she is a woman who needs response at the grown-up level.

P: (sadly) You don't really love me at all.
T: Hhmmnn.
P: You don't. You just don't care.
T: I'm helping you, am I not? Doesn't that seem like a good way to love somebody?
P: Oh, I don't *mean* like that! I mean me, me as I am, not somebody you're just . . . helping!
T: Well.
P: (beginning to weep) I want you to love me! I want you to love me, not just give me a lot of therapeutic double-talk!
T: I do love you.

This is true. T indeed has deep affection for P. But the mere sound of those words "I do love you" strikes fear into him. At first he feels only an undefined stab of anxiety. Within seconds he becomes self-conscious of his emotionality. He is apt, as are others, to confuse love with sexuality. If in fact he loves P, will this not lead to more complicated feelings? The specter of a damaging countertransference looms up before his eyes. Quickly, he must amend his statement:

T: I love the little girl in you.

The "little girl" in P is a creature of the past. She can hardly take comfort in such an abstract and, to her, "unreal" kind of offering. The past is far away. *Now* is when she needs it.

T, who had effectively affirmed her worthwhileness with his "I do love you," just as effectively destroys this affirmation by simply "loving the little girl" in her.

VIII. Games to Deny the Wish to Control

It is a basic fact in life that people seek to exert influence over others. A great deal of identification was evoked by Cole Porter's line: "I want to gain complete control of you . . . And handle even the heart and the soul of you . . ." The desire exists in therapy as well as in love.

On the other hand, many therapists, preferring to see themselves as superbly democratic and scientifically detached, fail to admit, frankly, their wish to influence interpersonal treatment situations. Added to this, they are sensitive to the accusation that they are "playing God." Steeped in admonitions against personal involvement, against "directiveness," T falls back on devices with which to hide a normal trait.

A. My Patient

The control-wish beneath the game of *My Patient* is evident in the possessive pronoun. This can be varied with *I Have a Patient Who . . . This Patient of Mine Said,* etc. The "I have," the "of mine," give the game away. If possession is indeed "nine-tenths of the law," it is at least seven-tenths of therapy. Rarely does T refer to P as "a patient" or "someone I know." The word "patient," however, tends to give the phrase professionality, which, in turn, indicates the absence of possessiveness. Therefore T does not often refer to P as "my meshugganah" or "my nudnick," either of which might in fact be a more appropriate appellation. If he does, it is usually outside the office. (See *Games Played Socially.*)

B. I Only Asked a Question

Analytic, or anti-action, therapists rely on the power of suggestion. For example, it would undercut the very foundations of classic theory and technique if T, confronted by a rigid and repressed P, said, "Go on out and get laid." For how, if T is that directive, will he bear the responsibility for the results? To choose the most extreme danger, there is always suicide. It has been said by at least one accredited, senior T that nearly all psychoanalysts who have practiced long enough are eventually faced with one suicide, and sometimes two.

An impatient T, eager to culminate a case successfully, aware that he might get it over with sooner by using control, and at the same time, wishing to deny his wish for that control, might say the following:

T: What do you think is really making you so frightened about sexual intercourse?

P: Well, we've done a lot of work on that. It's my mother. My mother used to tell me not to fuck girls because if I did I'd get into a lot of trouble.

T: What kind of trouble?

P: We've done that, too. She meant (a) it wasn't nice; (b) the girl could get pregnant; and (c) the girl's parents could make a terrible fuss about it.

T: Is that what scared you?

P: No. You know what scared me. I thought she meant I'd get hurt in some way; that my body would get—hurt.

T: Do you still believe that?

P: No, of course not.

T: So, in other words, now, today, there's really nothing stopping you?

P sees the reasonableness of this. He decides to take action. The following weekend he picks up a girl and goes to bed with her. She is beautiful, kind, and generous. He enjoys the act enormously and finds himself to be virile beyond his wildest dreams. Three days later he has gonorrhea.

P: (at his next therapeutic session) It's your fault. If you hadn't told me to . . . if you hadn't put me onto it . . .
T: I didn't tell you anything.
P: You said there was nothing to stop me!
T: *I only asked a question . . .*

C. You Are Responsible for Your Own Orgasms

Mary McCarthy to the contrary (*The Tyranny of the Orgasm*), it is assumed, and with probable validity, that American women have substantial trouble in reaching the sexual climax.

In the following example, P is a 35-year-old housewife. She is pretty, spirited, and truly desirous of expressing herself sexually. T has attempted for a year to bring P to an insight of her basic fear and dislike of men. He has convinced her that if she can view her husband with less timidity, with less bottled-up anger, the problem of her marital frigidity will be resolved. In putting forth these theories, he has been openly directive in his praise of men. He has met George. George is a warm and tender sort of man, is he not? Added to that, he is handsome. P has accepted T's suggestion. She decides to give it an all-out try by going with George on a "second honeymoon." She returns from the trip and hightails it back to T's office.

P: Well, it was lousy.
T: Why?
P: You . . . you build me up for a year with all this stuff. You make me think it's my problem. So second honeymoon. So big deal. Five hundred dollars down the drain on the lousiest weekend I ever had.
T: What happened?
P: I could hardly manage to get him into bed. It's Williamsburg; it's historical; he wants to go sightseeing. At night

he's so tired from sightseeing he can't see at *all*. I work on him. I do everything. Finally he gets it up, and then bang-bang-bang and it's over. Men . . .

T: What about you?

P: Me? I lay there like a dead fish with 200 pounds on me. A lot *you* know! You're a *man*.

T: Now, now, you are misplacing the blame. I was suggestive, but it's you who are responsible for your own orgasms . . .

The game can lead to complications. While T has absolved himself by denying his wish to control, and by dumping the failure back onto P, P has decided with a vengeance to *be* responsible for her own orgasms. First she becomes an A-one masturbator. Then she shares her discovery with the needy housewife next door.

D. Motivation

P: 1. I saw the parking space first, so I took it, and the other guy backed into me.

2. I wanted sex that night. But I was all sweaty from working all day, so I took a bath first, and he fell asleep.

3. I knew she was looking forward to seeing *Man in the Glass Booth*, but the tickets were last-row, so I took her to *Hello Dolly*.

4. I know he likes steak, but it was too late to go shopping so I gave him chicken à la king.

5. He was very tired when he came home, but I woke up the baby because he hadn't played with her all day.

T: Let's analyze your motivation . . .

Motivation is basic to all games in which T wishes to control, controls subtly, and then disclaims his part in the results. P can report all manner of mistakes, made through even the most acceptable circumstances, and T can remain safe behind the irrevocability of that one word.

E. We're Here to Analyze (or You're Acting Out)

The traditional T leads P to insight through verbal exchange. *Insight,* which in many cases is merely a euphemism for *hindsight,* piques P's desire to "act out." He is apt to say, "I'm fine now; I know enough; I want to do." T, in his classic training, has been taught the dangers of "acting-out," and must cope with the added burden of his responsibility for whatever hindrance, harm, or hysteria results from the active "doing" of P.

T is in a spot. He is, allegedly, a well-adjusted and well-analyzed person who is above making value judgments and is, consequently, in no position to say or feel that certain activities are "bad." He is, however, empowered, as an expert, to suggest that forbidden activity is "really" related to what P feels toward him through transference. On the one hand, he, too, wishes to direct P to a point where P can make his own decisions and live his own life. On the other hand, there are the "rules" and his dread of causing irreparable damage in P's psyche. It is safer, then, to direct P to an awareness that all activity is based on P's transference to T. In this case, the transference would be "negative."

The concept can be clarified by its comparison with a certain type of mother who sees herself at the center of the universe and judges the reactions of her children accordingly. If her daughter (D) likes the neighbor's son, this mother (M) tells her, "You only see him because you know I don't like him, and you're not happy unless you're making me miserable." If D refuses flatly to have anything to do with the neighbor's son, and has no better prospects at hand, M says,

"The only reason you sit at home is because you know I'm only living to see you meet a nice boy and get married."

When T admonishes P against acting-out, he is behaving in like manner. And, as is often the case in M's perversity, he wishes to control yet deny this, because of fear of the responsibility which is involved.

For P to continue his "acting-out" behavior in the face of such interpretations, he must accept the onus of being, at best, "uncooperative." Confronted with this, the less hardy P finds it easier to abandon the behavior. The bolder, more ego-fied P may choose to abandon the treatment.

Behavior which is commonly labeled "acting-out" includes:

1. dating someone of another race
2. dating someone of another religion
3. smoking pot
4. attending an orgy
5. changing jobs
6. marrying
7. divorcing
8. having a baby
9. growing a beard
10. affecting décolletage at 11:00 A.M.
11. publishing a personal account of psychoanalysis before (or after) being terminated

When P reports activity to T which has, in fact, been suggested by the course of therapy itself, T tells him, *"We are here to analyze."*

F.   I Didn't Dream It, You Did

In spite of T's wish to deny his wish to control, he does control. P is impressionable. It takes no more than the slightest hint from T to get him to incorporate the hint into his unconscious mind.

In the following verbal exchange, T is a male with hidden aggressivities. P is a young female, low on ego, who senses T's aggressivity, but is not yet aware of her wish to reciprocate in kind:

P: I woke up in the most awful sweat. It seems I was standing in an open field, alone. You were there, too, but I didn't see you. Suddenly you jumped out at me from nowhere and tried to rape me. I raised my arm to fend you off, but just at that moment you fell forward, missed me, and broke off your penis.

T: *I didn't dream it, you did.*

Denial of the wish to control is inextricably bound up with fear of taking the rap.

IX. Games to Deny Feelings of Superiority

Whether or not all men are created equal, it's a pretty sure thing that all of us think we are better than *some* others. At the very least we know that we can do certain things better than other people can do them. The history professor knows that he may not be as good with his hands as the local mechanic, but he believes he is better at teaching. There are therapists who have fallen for their own Public Relations: They feel quite superior to other human beings in a good many areas. Yet, at the same time, they pride themselves on their innate egalitarianism. This, quite naturally, results in a conflict. Guilty about their feelings of superiority, they deny them in games calculated to prove their democratic natures:

A. There Is No Difference Between Us

In reality, there are many areas in which T and P are similar. To begin with, they are both human beings. Perhaps they are of the same sex. Each shares an experience of treatment in that T, if he is a psychoanalyst, has undergone an analysis similar to the one P is now undergoing; if he classifies as another type of therapist he has likely been treated in the way that he must one day treat. Yet he is aware of his superiority through the virtues of time and experience with needful and confused people, and often he helps to remove that heavy halo from his head by forcing himself, falsely and without validity, down to P's level:

P: You know so much.
T: Well, not all that much.

P: You graduated from Harvard with honors.

T: Hhmmnn.

P: Then you went to P & S at Columbia.

T: Um.

P: Then you studied abroad with people who actually studied under Freud.

T: Well . . .

P: You've had nine books published.

T: Ah . . .

P: I went to P.S. 6, and then I barely made it through Eras-
mus High.

T: That doesn't matter, *there is no difference between us.*

This is a tricky game. Later, when P's ego has had an overhauling, and T is trying, earnestly, to offer P a dream-interpretation which is, in truth, more valid than P's own, P will remind him that they are equals.

B.   You Don't Say!

When T is really hard put to deny his feelings of superiority, he may ask P to tell him something about which he knows nothing. Say P is by profession an oceanographer or by avocation a light-plane pilot. T encourages P to speak of these skills. P, tired and distraught with months of dredging his soul, complies happily with an oration which lasts for twenty minutes. T asks for minute details, the answers for which only someone in P's field can answer. When P finishes, T says slowly, and with awe: *"You don't say . . .!"* The game has served to lessen T's superiority-guilt, and also to build P's ego. For this reason it cannot be considered a damaging game. At worst, time has been spent away from more pressing and relevant material; and even this may prove to be helpful in its way, since P's production may lead to relating free associations.

C. I Learn from My Patients

P comes to therapy with feelings of worthlessness. While he pays T well for treatment, he retains the notion that he is wasting T's time. To P, the exchange of value seems entirely one-sided; T gives, P takes. This "emotional error" offers T a fine chance to disabuse P of his egoless repsonse, at the same time relieving some of his superiority anxieties.

P: I'm boring you.
T: No.
P: How can you stand this tedious work?
T: Don't worry, I have my rewards.
P: Like what?
T: *I learn from my patients.*

D. One Day You Won't Need Me Anymore

Once more we are struck with T's resemblance to the Jewish Mother. In order to remove from himself the weight and responsibility of authority, and the guilt of the superiority complex, he turns to ploys of self-abnegation.

P: You're everything to me.
T: Oh, not everything.
P: Without you, where would I be?
T: Well, now . . .
P: If it weren't for you, I'd be done for. Think of me a year ago. Lost, miserable, suicidal . . . Nothing, and even now . . . if I didn't have you, could I go on?
T: (smiling, but with the faintest trace of sadness) Oh, you're better than you think you are. You'll see—*one day you won't need me anymore . . .*

The game is harmful on two counts:

    a. P, not nearly ready for termination, is struck down with panic at the mere idea of the inevitable separation from the one person who is making his blighted life worth living, and

    b. T's peek-through sadness evokes in P a pity and a compassion which further enslaves him. Like the son of a self-sacrificing mother, he vows within himself, "I will never leave you!"

E.   I Flunked Wood-Working 2

  P: I was terrible at school. I never did my homework, and I was left back three times. My mother was constantly having to come and see my teachers, and even after she got me a tutor, I got 54 on the Algebra Regents Exam!

  T: None of us is perfect. *I flunked Wood-Working 2.*

T, while attempting to lessen his superiority, is at the same time careful to confess a failure only in a most insignificant area. If P is sufficiently insecure, he will continue to berate himself. If he has, by this point, become sufficiently egofied, he will laugh out loud.

F.   Bathroom

Ps with heavy positive transferences invest in their Ts all manner of superhuman qualities. In our society, bathroom functions are looked upon with shame and embarrassment, as proven by the compulsion and anxiety with which mothers take on the toilet-training of their young. It is a rare adult American who is not, at some level, still hung up on residual memories of his "dirtiness" as a little child. It is natural, then, that we remove from our heroes and heroines the stigma of such base and unattractive functions as urination and defecation.

The T who is burdened with false superhumanness can smash P's fantasy by excusing himself to go to the bathroom, allowing P, if possible, to hear the tinkle of his urinary stream and roar of the plumbing.

There is no exaggeration in this example. Upon the return of her T from the bathroom, a P of three years' duration resumed her productions with, "My God! You really *do* it!"

A female T of proper age can further this smash by leaving her box of Tampax in view so that it can be seen by Ps who must, themselves, use the bathroom.

The game is an effective one with positive aspects.

X. *Games to Deny Feelings of Inferiority*

Games to deny feelings of inferiority and to keep actual inferiority from being exposed are of course games played to impress. As ambivalence dogs our human footsteps throughout life, causing us to love and hate simultaneously those who are related to us, so does it feed the inner conflict of self. While we believe that we are superior, we believe, at the same time, that we are inferior; and this dichotomy of responses is perhaps one of the most confusing and entrapping in the entire emotional scale. Therapists—educated, trained, and in a position of authority—are no less beset by fears of inferiority-exposure than other people; nor are their professional devices against such exposure less petty. We have all been children, under fire of admonition and criticism. Once, long ago, we muffed our lines in the school play, failed to impress someone with whom we desired friendship, put forth our left foot when in fact our right foot would have prevented our fall. Growing, we learned the complex mechanisms of defense, and the games calculated to raise us, in the eyes of others, above ignominity. The little boy walks the picket fence, calling "Look, Ma—no hands!" The little girl, cowed by the domineering mother, attempts to secure her own femininity by baking a batch of cookies long before she can read a recipe.

Therapists have at their disposal many gambits with which to accomplish the same ends.

A. Last Year at the Geneva Convention

In the following example, P, in treatment for several years, has reached a point of egofication which allows him to challenge T. It has occurred to P that T's training has had little to do with his basic intellect and intelligence. Given that training, P himself would, more than likely (he feels), have made the grade as well, even topped it with additional creativeness and originality.

When T's status is challenged, he falls back on the props of his professional experience. The prop he chooses may have no relation whatever to P's attack, but it will mitigate the loss by "making an impression."

P: You're not terribly perceptive at times.

T: Hhmmnn. How's that?

P: My dream. Your interpretation was pretty shallow. Pat stuff, right out of the book.

T: Yes?

P: Yes. The man on that lonely road, wearing the strange jester's costume and singing the inane little song . . . you said it was my father, whom I had at last seen as harmless and in fact a little ridiculous. Well, if you had had the perception to take it a step further, you might have concluded that since I am a part of my father, I see in his figure that man who is really me. It was my-self whom I met on that road—myself, whom I could at last face with acceptance and compassion . . .

T: *Last year at the Geneva Convention . . .*

B. As Otto Rank Once Said

This game is related to *Geneva Convention* in that it calls upon external forces for its impressiveness. When P challenges T's suggestions or statements, T identifies himself with another T of world renown in order to prove to P that he (T) travels, theoretically, in the very best of company:

P: My mother was a writer who wrote novels behind a locked door when she should have been taking care of me. Suddenly you're trying to get me to believe that she really loved me!

T: The creative personality is . . . well . . . as *Otto Rank
   once said* . . .

The game is likely to have ramifications. Many a P has
dabbled in the literature of psychiatry, and at the most
unexpected moments may hit T with a return serve-up of
Otto Rank.

C. It Sounds Like a Fugue by Bach

T, steeped in the reading matter of his own profession,
often finds himself at a loss for time in which to keep up with
the rest of "culture." P, aware of T's lack of general information, may play upon this lack, feeding T's frustration by
offering the most esoteric kinds of productions. T, noting the
subtle implication of his own inferiority, reaches far out into
left field for any *non*therapeutic frame of reference which
will prove his widespread range of interests and capabilities:

P: My moods follow a pattern of multiple levels. I can
   hear my despair rattling along on one level, while feelings of a completely different nature tinkle along at
   other levels, but all at the same time. So now (*with
   disdain*) I suppose you'll tell me I'm a "split personality"!

T: Not at all, not at all. I was simply going to say that
   it sounds like a fugue by Bach . . .

D. Big Words (and Bigger Words)

Most professionals incorporate their own languages. These
languages are in fact a kind of inner-sanctum code system,
meant, quite deliberately, to keep others out. The electronics
engineer can easily describe the simplest light bulb so that it
will be an unrecognizable object to all others present. In
doing so, he emphasizes the uniqueness of his position, his
special knowledge. Owing to the incredible vastness of psychiatric and psychologic literature, terminology has accrued
which is in itself endless. It might be said that professionals

in the human-relations field have at their command more special verbiage than any other group of communicating people.

The object of terminological usage is of course to impress, and this can be done effectively by complicating verbal matters to the utmost degree. What is in reality most simple, must be buried in ornateness so that outsiders may realize the difficulties Ts have mastered in their treatment and understanding of other human beings.

Here is a list of common words, used every day, by ordinary people—and their psychiatric substitutes.

personality, self	ego
conscience	super-ego
savagery	id
mixed up	neurotic
nuts	psychotic
silly	hebephrenic
split	schizophrenic
babyish	regressed
giddy	manic
suspicious	paranoid
isolated, uncommunicative	autistic
unscrupulous	psychopathic
creativity, energy	libido
responsive	empathic
cruel	sadistic
desire to suffer	masochism
forgotten	repressed
self-love	narcissism
eating pleasures	oral satisfaction
hang-up	fixation
person	object
sexuality	eroticism
fastidious	anal
fear	phobia

This list doesn't begin to make a dent in the translation of English into Freudilingua. This particular inner sanctum, however, has been sufficiently invaded by the Outs to rob it of most of its mystery. There are few people with any education at all who cannot use the aforegoing terms with as much ease and naturalness as any therapist.

Big Words, as a game, has lost a good deal of its impact. Ts and Ps who wish to keep a step ahead must begin to practice with *Bigger Words:*

emotional energy (applied to objects)	cathexis
confusion of present with past	parataxis
the whole, rather than its parts	Gestalt
representation of several people or feelings by one symbol	condensation
reliving of past emotion	abreaction
drowsiness	hypnogogia
masturbation	onanism, auto-eroticism
a mistake in action	*lapsus calami*
love of heirlooms	totemism
self-starvation	anorexia
sexual use of anus	pedicatio
lawful reproduction	exogamy
random sexual strivings	polymorphous-perverse
sexually infantile (female)	clitorid
fecal preoccupation	coprophilia
one troubled in specific situations	*hysterique d'occasion*
emotional paralysis	cataplexy
gruesome twosome	symbiotic relationship
action of a gruesome twosome	*folie à deux*
verbal urine hang-up	urilagnia
emotional or physical plateau	stasis
mother, father	archaic super-ego introjects

The following is a list of terms which have been dropped from the language by both T and P alike:

1. I'm very nervous today.
2. I was green with envy.
3. Don't aggravate me.
4. It's indigestion.
5. I didn't mean to interrupt you. (Or "I didn't mean" anything else.)
6. It was *only* a dream.
7. It was *just* an accident.
8. You're crazy.
9. I picked up a germ.
10. Chemistry.

E. Diploma

Diploma is a nonverbal game which depends solely on visual objects placed at strategic points in order to further substantiate P's impression of T. The framed, hung diplomas and degrees in T's office are only one of many prop-categories. Others include:

One large photograph of Sigmund Freud
A signed letter from Anna Freud
Bookcases
A revolving world-globe
A piece of pre-Columbian pottery
One signed graphic by Roy Lichtenstein
Reasonably up-to-date copies of:

1. *The Partisan Review*
2. *The New Yorker*
3. *Mad*
4. *Harper's Bazaar*

5. *Réalités*
6. *Art News*
7. *American Psychoanalytic Journal*
8. *Gourmet*
9. *True Confessions*
10. *The Village Voice*

True Confessions serves two purposes: (a) It proves T's superiority by demonstrating his acceptance, if not appreciation, of the commonplace; and (b) the title reminds P, unconsciously, of the task at hand.

F. Twenty Questions

The author of a detective novel knows, before he writes the book, precisely who committed the murder. Following his own plan he is able to build the story on a foundation of subtle clues; yet many a reader, not possessed of the mystery writer's particular type of mind and logic, is often held in complete suspense until the very end. "How," wonders the reader, "did he ever figure all that out?" Indeed the feat is an impressive one.

It is this same method which T employs when he treats P to a game of *Twenty Questions*. T knows ahead of time what the conclusion will be. He chooses questions which seem to have little to do with the case; but each one has its purpose in leading up to the denouement. When, finally, P sees the light, reaches, through subtle direction, the blinding-flash of insight which T has had in mind for him all along, he is duly impressed.

Here is a typical round of *Twenty Questions* based on T's foregone conclusion that P has retained, throughout his life, a residual, if unconscious, memory of that phenomenon which is known in Freudian analysis as *the primal scene.* (*The primal scene* is the tableau, whether actually seen, or fantasied from the hearing of sounds, of P's mother and father while they are engaged in sexual intercourse.)

1. T: So your family spent the summers on Long Island?

   P: Yes.

2. T: In a little cottage, yes?

   P: Yes, very small. We didn't have a steady maid in the summer, and I was the only child.

3. T: But you had your own room?

   P: Oh, yes. A tiny room. It was a tiny cottage.

4. T: In tiny summer cottages there aren't halls, usually, are there?

   P: No. All the rooms were on one floor, sort of scrunched together.

5. T: So your room was next to your parents' room?

   P: Yes. Separate doors, of course, but one wall separating them—I mean the two rooms . . . one wall.

6. T: This was an old cottage? Or was it one of the newer ones built in a development of many cottages like it?

   P: A development cottage. I remember that because in those days it was considered very modern.

7. T: So the construction of the cottage was flimsy? That is, it was, if modern and attractive, what is sometimes called "jerry-built"?

   P: Yes, I guess you could say that. Those places were only built for summer tenants. People didn't live in them all year round.

8. T: Did you used to sleep well on those vacations?

P: Not particularly. You'd think I would because I went swimming every day, and there were lots of other kids around to go bike riding with, and things. But I guess I was always overexcited or something. I remember I used to wake up with nightmares sometimes.

9. T: How did your mother and father react to being away on vacation? Were they relaxed . . . away from the city, at the shore?

10. P. Oh, they were great. My father loved it, especially. He worked awfully hard all year, and he really looked forward to getting that month "away from it all." He used to say, "Well, the heat's off. I'm my own boss now, and I'm gonna do anything I goddamn please." He had a fine time. Went fishing, boating, caught up on his reading, napped, went to bed early . . .

11. T: And how did your mother seem during those times?

P: She loved it, too. I guess she was pretty pleased because my father wasn't as tense as he usually was. She got a kick out of cooking him all the things he liked, and letting him mosey around and nap and things.

12. T: So, in other words, your parents were pretty relaxed?

P: Oh, very. Nothing like they were in the winter.

13. T: About those nightmares you mentioned . . . did you used to get up by yourself after you had them?

P: Sometimes. Sometimes I'd go into the kitchen and get a snack. Mostly, I was too scared, though. I'd just lie in my bed in the dark.

14. T: Where was your bed? Where in your room was the bed placed?

P: Against the wall. Lengthwise. You know, "flush" against the wall.

15. T: Which wall was that?

P: Let's see now . . . not where the windows were. And not the wall where the door was. The third wall was the one separating my room from the living room. It wasn't that one because I remember there was a chest of drawers there.

16. T: Ah. So your bed was placed lengthwise, or as you say, "flush against the wall" that separated your room from your parents' room? Against that wall . . . in a flimsily built little cottage at the shore? Summer tenants only, no one there in winter, so the walls were thin . . . ? Plaster walls? Or perhaps even something like partitions? Beaverboard, painted over? And you lay in your little bed . . . in the dark . . . tense, rigid, after your nightmare . . . a child alone, afraid to move . . . not making a sound?

P: (beginning to feel very sorry for himself) Yes. Alone. I can *feel* that now, all over again, as if it's happening now . . . I was so . . . *lonely* . . . They were together, of course—they had each other . . .

17. T: They "had" each other? Isn't that an interesting *pun* on something when you stop to think of it? You think about that now, all right?
(There is a pause of at least a full minute, as P *abreacts*—that is, reconstructs the scene and relives the feelings of the past in the present.)

P: My God, they "had" each other . . . I see what you mean! They honest-to-God *had* each other!

18. T: And you heard? Tell me, what did you hear? You heard the creaking of the mattress springs? You heard them talking?

P: The mattress springs! Up! Down! Up! Down! Creak! Squeal! And my mother! I heard my mother! She cried out! I swear to you, I heard her cry out! (He begins to weep.) "Now!" she cried. "Now! Now! NOOOOOWWWWWW!!!" And then, "Darling," "Darling," she moaned, "oh, darling, oh, darling, oh, darling. . . ." I couldn't bear it! I was alone! They didn't want me. I was their little boy, but they didn't want me! They had each other!

19. T: So you see now, don't you? You understand . . . ? What was your father doing to your mother?

P: (brokenly) *Taking her away from me!*

20. T: So you know now what you knew then, and forgot, as the years went on, burying it in your unconscious mind because it was too painful to remember? You realize now, at last, that you heard *the primal scene,* and pictured it all in your mind's eye, and could never bear again to recall it as it really happened . . . ? And that all your life you have felt that initial rejection, and hated your father because he "had" your mother and took her away from you—you, who were a lonely little boy?

P: (weeping inconsolably) Oh, that son-of-a-bitch, oh that bastard! I loved her, I loved her so much and he took her away, and she *let* him and she *liked* it! Oh, that sonovabitching big-balled prick of a fucking cuntsucker!!! I WANTED TO KILL HIM!!!

Aided by Kleenex and perhaps the warm and reassuring hand of T on his shoulder, P quiets down enough to leave the office under reasonable control.

Mission accomplished: T, having felt a bit inferior that

day, has proved, once more, his uncanny perception, his irrevocable powers of logic. P, a winner too, will speak of this hour that same night to a friend: "Christ, what a thing happened today! Screw 'transference'—I'm tell you, my analyst is a genius!"

XI. Games to Deny Rigidity

It is the rigidity in human beings which is most responsible for perpetuating their mental illness. Change, deviation from safe and trusted patterns of thought and behavior, leads to a malaise which varies with the individual's flexibility. Again, the important matter of *degree:* what, in fact, was the rigidity (or *anality*) imposed upon us in infancy by parents whose main mission may have been to create a neat, clean product of early toilet-training? Who was the teacher who taught us our first arithmetic; did she or did she not keep us in after school, or slap our wrists, when we added three and two and got six? Did our piano instructors insist on the playing of each note separately and perfectly? Did the family pediatrician instruct our parents to hold us strictly to regular bedtimes, scheduled and unvarying balanced meals? Were we made to nap from 2:00 P.M. to 3:00 P.M., bathe from 5:30 P.M. to 6:00 P.M.? Were we allowed one and only one radio or TV program, following dinner and homework? Were we trained to respect the code of manners and courtesy: "One says this, and not that. One *does* this, and not that."

America, the country of the Pilgrims, has not yet, for all her wealth and know-how, succeeded in shaking off the chains of puritanism. While, as a nation, we may *do* more questionable things than people of other countries, having the material means with which to get away with them, we sail largely on a subterranean river of guilt-feelings and maladjustments. Witness the emphasis placed on therapists and therapy. In some circles, admittedly those of the middle and upper classes, it is rare to come upon an individual who has not had at least some small brush with treatment.

116

Ts, like other people, must guard against the strangulation of inborn and intrained rigidity. And in so guarding, they turn to games which serve to prove their spontaneity.

A. Overtime

The most generally accepted time-span for a given therapeutic "hour" is fifty minutes. Some Ts have cut this down to forty-five minutes, a few, recently, to thirty minutes; others, trying new methods, have run their sessions out to double or triple the original time. In any case, whatever time has been allotted is usually maintained. The psychotherapeutic P, sitting up, knows that at a certain point in his verbal productions, the therapist will glance at his watch or clock, tap his fingers, or move about in his chair, all in the service of letting P know that his "time is up."

Accused often enough of robot-tactics, T is sensitive about his own rigidity and wishes to show that he is, in fact, a rather freewheeling individual. The wish is fulfilled on those days when he allows P to talk on for an extra five, ten, or fifteen minutes.

B. Lateness

When T plays *Overtime,* it is very likely that the P scheduled for the next session will be left sitting in the waiting room, biting his nails and feeding his hostility. This is particularly true for Ps who must return to their jobs, or meet other commitments. Such a P will enter T's office with a storm of protest, which T, due to his need to prove flexibility in his own makeup, will treat with a quiet, relaxed good humor:

P: You're running late again! I've been sitting out there for hours!

T: Well, not hours—a few minutes at the most.

P: I haven't got "a few minutes" to spare. I'm due back at the office on the dot of 1:25 today. What's the matter with you? Can't you keep to a schedule? Why are you always late?

T: Come, come . . . we aren't meant to be automatons, you know. We must learn to adjust to small changes when they appear to be called for . . . Too much *anality* isn't good for us.

P: I don't know. It seems to me *I* can manage to be on time, so why can't you?

T: Remember that you, too, have been allowed to stay a short while longer at times, and the patient following *you* has had to wait.

C. So What?

The P being treated by a T who is trying to deny his own rigidity is often in for a surprise. Say, for example, the pattern of therapy has been going along at a pretty consistent pace. P has continued to offer the same productions of free association and dream material for some months, while T has continued to place stress on the importance of certain serious interpretations. Suddenly, T, tiring of this endless consistency, changes hats, so to speak:

P: Like you tried to tell me, what I really feel is self-loathing. It's for that reason that I do these awful things to hurt myself. Only this morning, before I thought about it and got this important insight, I ran a bath without turning the cold water on. Then, not even testing it for temperature, I plunked myself right in and nearly burned my ass off.

T: *So what*?

D.   Take a Chance

This is another change-of-hats type of game which takes P by surprise and proves T's ability to switch attitudes in midstream. For months P has been cautioned by T to refrain from acting-out on wild impulses. P's ill-considered dives into activity have, it has been proven, only led to further problems: guilt feelings, recriminations from his wife, and the prolonging of treatment. He has learned the danger of this style of behavior, and respects T for his encouragement to be more cautious. Now he begins his hour in the throes of a new situational conflict:

P: My wife has invited her mother for the weekend again. That's the fourth weekend in two months, and I can't stand it anymore. I was just thinking . . . maybe I ought to have it out with her . . . my mother-in-law, I mean. She's a member of the WCTU and the word "darn" gives her a heart attack. If she thought for a minute we didn't run our house and bring up the kids according to *her* standards, she'd probably never set foot in the door again. I know I can't do it, of course, but I was thinking how great it would be if when she asked me to stop smoking because it's a "disgusting habit," I just looked up at her and said, "Go fuck yourself."

T: Why not . . . *take a chance*?

T has thus demonstrated his ability to be flexible. Should P, having taken this chance, return for his next hour with the news that both his mother-in-law and his wife have left forever, T can always play a round of *I Only Asked a Question* or *Motivation*.

E. Four-Letter Words

In most kinds of therapy, but particularly in deep analysis, there is a free use of four-letter words. That this "vulgarity" exists as part of an accepted and revered science, among supposedly sensitive and well-educated people, still comes as a surprise to many who have not themselves been patients. Yet we do know that the essence of successful therapy lies in the freedom to express oneself in any and all terms which cross the mind and the imagination. To shout SHIT! in the midst of a meeting at the First Presbyterian is equivalent to throwing a stink-bomb into a crowded theater: It is a breach of both manners and fairplay; it bespeaks a stupidity; it is uncivilized.

In therapy, however, civilizedness, even civility, is not the issue. The point is to discover Self in order that Self may first be accepted, and then be brought into change. And while sticks and stones do break bones, words are symbols of feelings. They hurt no one, and the more direct they are, the better.

Another, and far less beneficial, motivation for the use of such speech is based in the wish to *appear* emancipated. Here we have the little boy who is hell-bent on shocking his elders by proving his freedom from their strict standards. At the age of five he may enter his mother's Woman's Club session stark naked. Later he may chalk the word FUCK on a corridor wall in his elementary school. He is not "bad." He is merely a child, being childish.

The therapist, equally hell-bent on denying his rigidity, may play the same game.

There are times when P, having already accepted his own human fantasies or expressions of the "obscene," finds himself in a situation which truly evokes his more poetic leanings. Say he has just fallen in love with a girl who, at least for the time being, seems to be the answer to all his prayers. Quite naturally, her image moves into his therapy. He wants, and needs, to describe her:

P: We rode our bikes out into the country. The day was warm, and the perspiration on her upper lip was like dew touching the petal of a rose. When we stopped to have our boxed lunches, I held her in my arms and she smelled like new-mown hay. Then she went off into the woods, and I thought of dryads . . .

T: (about to play) What did she go off into the woods for?

P: (hesitating) I don't know.

T: Sure you know. You're repressing.

P: Repressing what? I'm telling you how it all struck me, I'm telling you my feelings about it.

T: Whatsa matter you can't discuss human functions.

P: But I can, it's just that . . .

T: Everybody shits and takes a leak, you know.

P: Do you have to put it that way when I'm . . .

T: How you put it isn't the point. The point is why certain words upset you. Why?

P: I don't know, right now they just . . . bother me.

T: You were taught they're bad, so now you're uptight about them. But you see, don't you, they don't bother *me*.

T has now shown P what a free-flying character he is. No nets for *him*. He got all that "crap" fixed up in his own analysis; he's been Saved. P, on the other hand, has just had one of his loveliest, and least harmful, fantasies hobnail-booted to death.

For T to open up P to an unrigid expression of life is

constructive. What is destructive is T's insistence on certain types of expressions for the mere purpose of denying his own rigidity.

XII. Games to Deny Lack of Discipline

While rigidity is a characteristic which is harmful to the self, lack of discipline, or the inability to keep organized, causes problems both for the self and for others. Many Ts feel that it is essential to present a front which is well-balanced between spontaneity and planned organization. At such times when T has a deep desire to let things slide, to hover pleasantly in the limbo of vagueness and irresponsibility, he pulls his reins in sharply, drawing himself back to the job at hand. A T who lacks discipline sets a bad example for his Ps who may either criticize him or imitate his laxness to the point where they miss sessions, arrive late or offer loose-witted and disconnecting verbal productions. In order to deny the wish to meet life on a what-the-hell basis, T constructs a number of devices to prove that he is in fact a very busy and well-oriented individual:

A. Telephone

There are some therapists, particularly in the psychoanalytic category, who, for the purpose of preventing interruptions in their Ps' free associations, turn off their phones during analytic sessions. Messages are taken by an answering service while small red or white lights go on and off to let T know that he is to check in for them. Most therapists, however, allow calls to come through while they and their Ps are working.

The receiving of outside communications has many advantages, mainly for T. For one, it breaks the tedium. For another, it gives T a chance to come back to P's productions with a fresh view. Most important, it allows T to demonstrate to P how busy he is, how necessary it is for him to handle conflicting problems and influences simultaneously and with a maximum of care and organization.

A T who is trying to impress his P in this fashion may sound as follows:

> "Oh, Nancy, yes . . . Last night? I see . . . And what did you tell him? Hhmmnn. Really? And how did you feel after you said it? Um. Well, you know what I told you . . . yes, about aggressivity. Yes. Yes. Well, Nancy, you can't blame him, can you? Hhmmnn. Yes. No. No, not tomorrow. All filled for tomorrow . . . unless you want to come at 7:00 A.M. . . . No, no, I'm up early. No, no, not at all. Do my reading and writing from 5:00 A.M. on. Well, you come then and I'll see you. Yes. Don't do it again tonight, Nancy. No. No, that wouldn't be wise. Yes, see you in the morning . . ."

P, lying on the couch, is awed by this transaction. Here T has been concentrating on P's timidity and lack of self-assertiveness, and right smack in the middle of it, Nancy, whoever the hell *she* is, calls up and obviously hits him with the problem of aggressiveness. How does T do it? He must have the mind of a smooth, well-oiled machine . . . And up at 5:00 A.M.! Good God, the discipline of it all . . .

B. Appointment Schedule

Ps asking to break already set appointments, or to arrange for extra ones, are usually kept waiting while T refers to his schedule. There is something sacred about this little book which is kept in view at all times, on T's desk, if not in his lap. It is not only an organized record of who will arrive and when; it is also the record which T uses at the end of the month when he or his secretary must make out his bills. Once in a while a P is charged for an hour which was in fact taken by someone else, but this is rare. The book is carefully kept, and this cannot help but impress P with T's standards as a self-disciplinarian.

In the case of new Ps, or would-be Ps, who telephone T for an initial appointment, T uses his schedule to a fare-thee-well:

Would-be P: (calling in February) Dr. Jones? You were recommended to me by a friend of mine who used to be your patient. I'm in a bad way. I'm depressed. I may commit suicide.

T: Hhmmnn. Let me look at my schedule . . .

P: It's urgent, Dr. Jones . . . I'm about to go right into the bathroom and slit my wrists.

T: Here, here we are. Well, now . . . I seem to be all booked up for the time being. Could you call me again at the end of May . . . ?

In truth, there is hardly ever a time when T cannot fit in one more urgent case. He can begin earlier in the day or work later on into the night. The would-be P needs only one visit, which is called an *evaluation*. If, after that session, T is actually "booked up," or decides he does not want to handle this particular case, he can refer the individual to another therapist. But T is trying to convince himself of his enormous busy-ness, and the would-be P must be shown, in spite of the rejection factor inherent in the put-off, that he cannot just barge in and expect the Schedule to be upset for his sole benefit.

Appointment Schedule is one of the most vicious games

going. A potential P thinks hard and long before he is able to face the shame and fright of telephoning a T. He does not call at the peak of joy but rather from the depths of serious depression.

Fortunately, and as T knows, the percentage of suicide threats in America far outdistances the percentage of suicides. The chances are good that the potential P will either live *through* his depression, live *with* it until the end of May, or telephone the therapist of another good friend. In the case of this last decision, T has the added advantage of being reported to be a very busy man with a Very Full Schedule.

C. Notebook (replay)

The game of *Notebook,* often played for the purpose of denying feelings of guilt over fees, can be replayed to deny lack of discipline. As T records, with his aforementioned scratchy pen, all that P is saying to him, he is setting up a ready file of P's productions. Case histories are surprisingly similar in basic content. After all, there are few of us who have not been born from the union of mother and father. It is quite possible for T to confuse one patient with another if he is going through a particularly schlublike period. *Notebook* is a great help at such times, and serves a second purpose—that of impressing P.

XIII. Games Played with Second-Rounders

For therapists, second-rounders are the icing on the therapeutic cake, the lovely gift-wrapped surprise at the very bottom of the Christmas stocking; in toto: the answer to the professional's prayer.

Second-rounders are Ps who have already undergone deep analysis. They have spent from three to five years on the couch of another T, have learned the rules and regulations of classical therapy, have come to the end of their tedious run-downs of the agonizing Past, and, like April, have laughed their girlish laughter, wept their girlish tears. Yet therapy knows no *real* end. For how perfectly "well-adjusted" can anyone be who has not settled for the problemless resolution of the grave? Therapy is a tool which, when handed over to P by T at termination-time, should be used by P, on his own, for the rest of his life. However, there is frequently a set of residual areas of nonresolution the treatment for which calls for one more go-round under the direction of a pro. Often psychoanalysis itself forms and leaves a subtle accrual of its own problems:

a. An unresolved transference to the former T which, uncompleted, unfinished, troubles the terminated P, overly influences his life functions, bugs his freedom, and continues to haunt him much in the way his archaically introjected parents once did.

b. Areas of neurosis, repressed during therapy either by P's inability to face them or by T's own "blocks," continue to fester, grow, and cause emotional and behavioral problems within a year or so of termination.

c. "Insights" gained during therapy turn out to have been invalid. Often a P is forced to an ideological conclusion by T's subjective direction and by P's need to "placate" him.

For these and many other reasons (loneliness, further need for authority figures, fear, the realization that a former T could not, philosophically, meet the personal standards of his patient, the desire to check things out from another point of view) P decides to "go back" into therapy with another T.

This second-round T is in an advantageous position, to say the least. The groundwork has been laid for him. He is free to play games which bring about fast and salubrious results. And the name of the major game is, of course—

A. Hail the Conquering Hero

Where T-1 has failed, T-2 will be victorious.

P, arriving in T-2's office for the first time, will be quick to show T-2 all that he has learned. He will display his hard-earned knowledge of Oedipal Conflict, Birth Trauma, Penis Envy, Castration Fear, Bi-Sexuality, Anxiety, ad infinitum. T-2, like the dentist who must always decry the work done by the dentist before him and replace all old fillings with new ones, will smile solicitously and play:

1. Dig Deeper

Dig Deeper impresses P. He has, after all, assumed that T-1 has covered all possible basic ground, and has dug deeply enough. That T-2's sensitivity, perception, and therapeutic know-how necessitates P's going several steps further at once dismays him and opens the valves of his admiration.

T-2: No, it is not enough that you know you were caught in an emotional vise between your mother and your father and, due to your mother's strength, took sides with your weak father and were then incapable of transferring from him to another man in marriage. If this were all there was to it, you would now be married. Obviously, something is still missing. We must *dig deeper* . . .

P: (several months later) Ah, I see it now . . . It wasn't just my mother's domination over my father which caused me to identify with him. It was also her frigidity, her dislike of men. She fostered an emotionally incestuous relationship between me and my father in order to spare herself the wife-role. In effect, she *married me off to him,* and from then on, I was unable to get an emotional divorce from him in order to marry someone else.

2. *You're a Victim of Countertransference*

As we have already emphasized, countertransference is the crime of technique. What better way for T-2 to abolish the theories of T-1 than by pointing out the presence of this misdemeanor:

P: I don't know why I feel so awful. After all, I had a perfectly good transference to Dr. X. I was "in love" with him for about three years, but he handled it beautifully. He never made me feel it was hopeless, or ridiculous—or that he was emotionally unattainable—which, of course, would have made me love him all the more. He was, if anything, too nice at times. Like the time I was crying about something and he got up from his chair and sat beside me on the couch and told me I was really very beautiful . . . I mean, I was certainly pleased, and all . . . but after that it seemed we weren't getting any-where. Every time I'd cry, he'd sit on the couch and pat my leg or something, and somehow I forgot what I was saying; or, maybe, what I was saying seemed to be sort of beside the point.

T: Well, *I'll be frank with you* . . . Dr. X is an excel-lent therapist, but I happen to know he is a rather old man who proves virility via his attraction to younger women . . . Obviously, *you are a victim of countertrans-ference* . . .

3. *I'll Be Frank with You*

I'll Be Frank with You is one of T-2's favorite games to play with second-rounders. As illustrated above, it fits into almost any situation. P, tired of years of therapy with T-1 who was not at all frank, but instead maddeningly mysterious at every possible turn, welcomes with relief T-2's openness. To be frank with someone is to let him in on a little secret. Little secrets are, in essence, little gifts which are bestowed upon special people who are grown-up enough to understand. P's ego soars; also, he tells his friend what a Great Guy T-2 is.

The following is a list of examples in which T-2 emerges as Frank and therefore as a Great Guy:

1. I had a patient in 1953 who committed suicide.
   Ya can't win 'em all, I always say . . .
2. Dr. Y is having trouble with the Institute.
   Too aggressive . . . When you get to know her, she turns out to be a pretty masculine woman . . .
3. The theory of Penis Envy is slightly debatable.
   Viola Klein, Karen Horney, and Gregory Zilboorg challenged Freud on the grounds that it isn't so much

a question of penis envy in women as it is of *envy of motherhood* in men . . .

4. I caught this damned cold I've got from not loving myself enough . . .

5. There's a lecture being given on this same subject we're discussing here, next Friday night, and I may be able to get a ticket for you . . .

6. Your husband's analyst was a patient of mine, and he's got a basic antipathy for women . . .

7. My son smokes pot.

4. *Stop Worrying*

It has been incumbent upon P, under the direction of T-1, to worry for five years. Nothing P said or did was ever taken at face value or interpreted as anything but of the utmost importance. There was the time when P tried to open T-1's office door in order to leave at the end of the session, and the door stuck. As a matter of fact, the knob was broken. But T-1 had been quick to tell P that P was, in "reality," averse to leaving because he "wanted to stay in the womb."

T-2 needn't work that hard. Nor need P. Deep analysis has already been undergone and, supposedly, terminated. Second-rounders usually come back for what might be thought of as a simple clean-up job, the tying in of a few loose ends.

P, however, used to the analytic approach, knowing the emotional significance of even the smallest and seemingly "accidental" acts, presents T-2 with all manner of careful self-interpretations:

P: 1. I got impatient with the driver ahead of me while I was coming down here. I honked my horn and nearly ran into him from behind. I suppose this

means I have a hidden desire to bugger somebody . . .

2. Last night my wife asked me to pass her the sugar,
   and I passed her the salt. Do you think maybe I'm
   still hostile to my mother?
3. There's a girl in my office who was having trouble
   making columns of figures, so I lent her my ruler.
   Am I a Lesbian?
4. Why do I wear dark glasses?
5. Do you think this tie is sort of faggy?
6. Last night I dreamed I was having another baby.
   Am I trying to prove my femininity?

To any of these productions, T-2 is able to respond
with: *Stop worrying* . . . It then begins to occur to P that
life may indeed be a breeze after all . . . but would he ever
have known it if it hadn't been for T-2's attractive and
endearing simplicity?

XIV. Games Played with Other Therapists

Therapists shall be considered to be playing games with one another when the content of what they communicate to their colleagues is less important than the purpose behind the communication.

A. Practice-Building Games

Psychoanalysts, psychiatrists, and various of their lesser counterparts are like other top professionals in that they are too proud to go begging for work and too "ethical" to advertise. To make an open request to a fellow therapist for patient-referrals is likely to backfire in any case because it will lead to the question, "What's wrong with X that he can't keep a good practice going?" Practice-building games are designed to overcome this difficulty through their indirectness of approach. They are likely to bring in new patients without placing T in the shameful position of having to resort to open solicitation.

1. Cocktail Party

The game of Cocktail Party consists in T's inviting prominent colleagues to his home for a "casual affair." In point of fact, the only casual aspect of this game lies in the off-handed style of the invitation. T's wife, if he has one, drops cute notes to prospective guests no earlier than two weeks before the chosen date. Telephone calls will do as well, particularly if the invitation is slipped in as an afterthought: "Oh, I meant to tell you—we're having some people over on the 27th . . ."

Included on the guest list are a number of noncolleagues whose purpose will be explained subsequently. Milling crowds are avoided because they tend to depersonalize the atmosphere and to devalue the importance of those present.

a. *Guest List*
   4 to 6 colleagues and their wives or escorts
   1 artist and his wife
   1 musician and his wife
   1 novelist and his wife (nonfiction writers are less effective since it is harder for guests to assume that their work is autobiographical)
   1 poet and her poems
   1 businessman and his wife (preferably one who collects paintings or graphics)
   1 politician (or historian) and his wife
   2 Negroes and their wives: one white, one black
   1 male homosexual and his boyfriend
   1 hippie and his teenybopper (preferably T's own son)
   1 top career woman and her husband or escort
   1 top career woman, unescorted
   1 or 2 relatives (preferably immigrant in-laws with foreign accents)
   1 female Pakistani wearing a sari
   2 dullards

This guest list is compiled by T to impress his colleagues (C) with his capacity for friendships with a variety of social types, his general conviviality, and his lack of overselectivity. In actual fact, each guest serves a well-considered purpose: The presence of cultured persons such as painters, musicians, and writers proves T's sensitivities, education, and breeding; businessmen prove T's respect for the value of the dollar; politicians and historians show that T is conscious of the world about him; Negroes eliminate the doubt of racial prejudice; homosexuals prove that T is unthreatened by his own latency; hippies and teenyboppers prove that T has bridged the generation gap; career women prove that T has resolved his castration anxieties; sari-clad Pakistanis are exotic; unseemly relatives prove that T has faced reality; dullards prove that T has indeed been free of connivance in the compilation of his guest list.

b. *Notes for the Hostess*

(1) T's wife buys an elegant but simple dress or pair of party-pants. When C comments favorably, she says, "Thank you *so* much . . ." "What, this old thing?" and "I designed it myself" are trite and obvious.

(2) In the matter of food, she has two choices; she can order elaborate hors d'oeuvres from a good caterer or spend the better part of three days and nights making them herself. In either case, when C pays hommage, she says, "I'm so glad you're enjoying them . . ." Whether or not she has made them remains a mystery. If C persists in asking, it is only to trap her—so she cuts that game by telling the truth.

(3) In the matter of liquor, she sees to it that booze is plentiful and varied. If C should want a Black Russian or a Bull-Shot, there should be no question of the availability of wine, beef broth, or large black olives. Also, bartenders and their assistants are definitely IN: There is nothing so unattractive

and disconcerting to guests as having their host and hostess *potchkying* around with glasses and loaded ashtrays like a couple of *oysgehmitchitehs*.

c. *Conjoint Preparations*

(1) T and his wife (or hostess) rest before the party, or, better still, make love. This reduces their tensions, adds glow to the skin, and gives them a united front.

(2) T and wife (W) lecture their younger children as follows:

(a) "Be open and friendly to everybody, but don't hang around too long."

(b) "You may say Hell and Damn, but not Fuck unless it is essential."

(c) "Do not wander quietly about with a load in your pants."

(d) "Do not tell Dr. X what we said about him last night."

(e) "Use everyone's proper name, or if you can't remember it, no name at all. Do not call anyone Rat-Fink, Shrink, or Shit-head."

(3) T and W practice calling each other Darling—but not too often. Overuse will be recognized as a cover-mechanism for hatred.

The game of *Cocktail Party* is relatively harmless to patients, who are not usually invited. If, however, a P of extreme insecurity or paranoid tendency is informed of the activity via a friend, he will go straight to pieces.

2. *Lunch Hour*

Lunch Hour is a popular game among young attending physicians at large psychiatric hospitals who are eager to establish their private practices.

Outline

a. T chooses a seat at a table where one or more senior therapists (ST) are eating, while his younger colleagues lunch down the hall.

b. A minimum age-gap of fifteen years should exist between T and ST.

c. ST, flattered by this attention, becomes a potential benefactor, or good-father-surrogate, while T must convey to his older host the impression of a precocious but quiet and admiring son.

d. ST asks T if T has any time available for a patient ST has seen in consultation.

e. T, suitably pleased and surprised, thanks ST, and humbly asks for ST's opinion of the case.

f. ST says, "Mother Fixation—you'll find it an interesting challenge."

g. A few days later T sees the referred P. She is 51; unmarried; over the past twelve years she has seen six other Ts; she can afford only one session a week at $10.

h. T writes ST a note in which he thanks him for a most fascinating referral.

i. T returns to the dining room and sits at the table of another potential benefactor.

Lunch Hour is rarely played in outside restaurants by practicing Ts with full schedules. Munching a lettuce-tomato-and-bacon on toast to the knocking of ice in a container of coke during a midday session is preferable to wasting an hour's worth of fee. In addition, it is a game similar to *Bathroom*, which helps P to realize that T is "human."

3. *Weekend Guest (Coming and Going)*

Weekend Guest (Coming) is a more elaborate version of *Cocktail Party* and can be played only by Ts who live in the suburbs or the country. The strains of creating a favorable impression over an entire weekend demand that the game be reserved for extra-special guests, such as:

1. the director of T's psychoanalytic institute
2. the chief of service of the hospital with which T is affiliated
3. the director of a large consultation service
4. any ST with potential benefactor tendencies

Those of lesser rank can just as readily be treated to a round of *Cocktail Party*.

Rules for *Cocktail Party* apply, in general, to *Weekend Guest (Coming)* in the matter of decent food. But it should be served with an off-hand flexibility. Of the two or three nights in question, at least one should include a local restaurant noted for its regional menu.

Added local color can be offered by the "dropping in" of a couple from down the road, preferably a gentleman farmer and his rotund, simple-minded wife. The burden of unrelenting shop talk is mitigated by a "real woman" type who is versed in popover recipes and the birthing of calves.

Clothes for *Weekend Guest (Coming)* should include well-planned "casuals." For T, weather permitting, a woodsman's jacket, checked red and black, and a hunting cap from Abercrombie and Fitch, the flaps of which are worn down over the ears. (Clothes for the T on the professional Make forms a section in itself, for, suffice it to say, the old Madison Avenue slogan "Dress British, Think Yiddish" applies to men of therapy as well.)

In late fall or winter, fires in fireplaces are essential.

If possible, logs used for same should come from T's own dead trees which he has, presumably, chopped up by himself. Ruddy complexions can be achieved by the borrowing of T's wife's facial sauna, if she has one.

The role of T's wife can be likened to a crayon sketch by Picasso: "A child could have done it . . ." except, of course, that a child could not have done it in a million years. T's wife plans ahead for the most easy-going attitudes possible. In the case of pools (often they are constructed personally with the aid of a rented bulldozer and steam shovel), bikinis are In, provided her figure allows for them. In winter, daytimes call for blue jeans and a disarming old sweatshirt. The woman who lolls around in a pants-suit from Bergdorf's is obviously *anal* in other areas of her life, if not actually frigid. Yet to be an out-and-out slob is to evince indications of a lack of healthy narcissism. The sweatshirt should be laundered.

Weekend Guest (Going) involves all the regulations of *Weekend Guest (Coming)* (casualness, absence of rigidity), plus the giving of the Gift. Clay ashtrays made by children at Nursery School are Out. Steuben glass is extremely expensive and indicates insecurity. A happy medium can be struck by Orifors or its copies. Records are always In. Rare is the T or the ST who would be caught dead without Stereo. Choices might include *Om,* a recent recording of Eastern music with an accompanying dissertation on Life (in English), Woody Allen, Bob Dylan, Dylan Thomas reading *Under Milkwood,* Dick Gregory, or a way-out stab with Anna Russell performing from *The Ring.*

For children, "creative" toys smack of clinicalism. It is best to give them something nontherapeutic, even antitherapeutic, such as an art book. They may not like it, but their parents will.

4. *Messrs. Brooks Brothers, Abercrombie and Fitch*

As has been mentioned, "Dress British, Think Yiddish" is a good rule of thumb for Ts. Indeed, a T's choice of clothes is not an easy one. While Pierre Cardin is a fine designer for STs in their off-duty hours, a Nehru jacket and medallion would not become a man who has taken it upon himself to cure the emotional ills of the world. Nor, on the other hand, should his clothes be tasteless. It is not below a female P, caught in the throes of a negative transference, to latch her grievances on to the atrocious ties worn by her T. A clever T will remind her subtly of the episode in *A Clearing in the Woods:* Virginia demonstrates her Oedipal Conflict by cutting her father's tie into small pieces. Most Ts, however, would not be familiar with the play, and must rely on less esoteric measures.

Rooster Ties will pass, although a discerning P will see them as common and middle class.

While Brooks Brothers, Abercrombie and Fitch are clothiers of the Establishment, they do produce suits and jackets which *fit*. Sports coats, particularly cashmere ones, are also Establishment, but they add an air of both success and flexibility.

Female Ts have an easier time of dressing. Tailored suits and shirts with cuff links bespeak masculinity, but a female T can impress an ST with what might even be considered "overdressing" by fashion connoisseurs. In our society the problem is for females to stay feminine (Betty Friedan to the contrary), and the wearing of elegant clothes and good jewelry will be accepted by ST as a manifestation in T of her healthy instincts. At the same time, she is setting a good example for her female Ps, who often, due to lack of ego, begin their courses of therapy looking like refugees from the Army-Navy Surplus Store.

5. *My Wife*

Regardless of T's personal stature in his field, the moment when he is called upon to say, ". . . and this is *my wife*" is the Moment of Truth. For it is T's choice of mate which exposes his entire basic male makeup as it bears upon his earliest relationships with Mother and Father.

The T who is married to an extremely "sexy" woman, one who is overcosmeticized and wears tight, sleezy dresses, is obviously insecure about his ability to cope with a "real" woman. There is some question these days as to what a "real" woman really is, but it should go without saying that most chorus girls have never achieved orgasm.

On the other hand, the T whose wife is of the Army-Navy variety is apt to be accused of dodging the male-female issue altogether. It can be said of him that he has married the next best thing to a young boy.

Some Ts marry, with either conscious or unconscious deliberation, the nurses they have met while in training at medical or mental hospitals. In these cases there is little danger of being dominated either emotionally or intellectually.

The T who marries another T is able to instill in his patients and colleagues the fantasy of the Perfect Relationship. After all, what marital secrets are there in this world of which a T-plus-a-T are not fully aware? The validity of this concept can, however, become questionable when the offspring of these unions are examined. Usually, and for some still-mysterious reason, the children of two Ts, particularly psychoanalysts, are veritable bats out of hell.

The game of *My Wife* is most convincingly played when T is able to introduce a woman who most closely meets the following qualifications:

1. attractive

2. approximately five years younger than T
3. post-college career in the field of publishing, music, or communications
4. present career of Mothering, for three children
5. psychoanalyzed, with honorable discharge
6. an inch or so shorter than T
7. heiress to legacy of a successful doctor-father (arbitrary)

While Ts are admired by other Ts for their choice of reasonably challenging women, there is yet more praise for the one who selects the kind of woman who "won't give him any trouble."

For a female T, the choice of mate is, as in the matter of dressing, far more simple. She can marry a man who does anything, provided he does it very, very well.

B.   Discrediting Games

Discrediting Games are played by Ts with other Ts in order to establish superiority.

1. *Superficial*

T-1: How's that knotty case coming?
T-2: New wrinkle. Obesity.
T-1: So what do you think brought it about?
T-2: She doesn't have the narcissism to overcome her need for oral satisfaction.
T-1: *Superficial.*

Any careful analysis of *Superficial* leads to the conclusion that T-1's aim is to discredit T-2's intelligence and competence. If this weren't the case, T-1 could just as well offer his own interpretation of the case instead of first soliciting T-2's. Or in the final verbal exchange, he could as readily say, "I've got another idea of what it might mean."

In most psychological situations phenomena can be viewed legitimately from several points of view; it would be difficult to decide which view was deeper, and which more superficial. We can assume, then, that when T-1 calls T-2's interpretation "superficial," he really means "ridiculous." However, professional ethics and artfulness mitigate against such bluntness. To evince the latent hostility underlying the word "ridiculous" is to invite an accusation of Countertransference.

Indeed, T-1's position is similar to that of the legendary blind man who argues with another blind man about the elephant. When T-2 touches the tusk and says, "An elephant is hard and thin like a bone," T-1 touches the leg and says, "Superficial! It is fat and round like a tree!"

2. *Countertransference* (*replay*)

Countertransference, the bane of all Ts' lives, is used as a game when T-1 employs it as an accusation against T-2. For this accusation challenges more than transient wisdom; it casts serious doubt on T-2's emotional stability and questions the value of his $25,000 five-year personal analysis.

> T-1: How's that female patient you were telling me about?
> T-2: Coming along.
> T-1: You didn't resolve the obesity problem?
> T-2: I'm putting it off for a while. I figure it's hard enough for her to gain insight about her lack of ego without suggesting a crash-diet at the same time . . .
> T-1: *Countertransference!*

Those Ts who play *Countertransference* with other Ts assume that the only valid attitude toward any P is one of total neutrality and objectivity; that any emotional response on the part of a T is due to his involvement with P due to P's having "become" his mother, father, sibling, friend, or lover. In other words, should T respond humanly to the human being whom he is treating, he is presumed neurotic.

To avoid the accusation of *Countertransference,* T should follow two suggestions:

a. When speaking of a P, never admit to feeling:

bored
angry
tired
loving
lustful
depressed

b. When speaking of a P, never admit to acting:
curtly
aggressively
critically
solicitously
jokingly

Should a T still be charged with *Countertransference,* his only recourse is to turn the tables on his accusor and challenge him to a game of *Superficial.*

Master *Countertransference* players are generally clever and intelligent, but basically unresponsive people. They are the spectators of life rather than the participants, and even socially they are unwilling to risk the charge of "excessive emotionality." Prone to flattery, they are readily susceptible to *Lunch Hour,* but it is wise to refrain from playing *Cocktail Party* with them since they add about as much gaiety as an IBM Computer.

3. *Unconventional*

Certain situations arise in which T-1, speaking to a mixed audience of laymen and professionals, wishes to cast doubt upon T-2 among his colleagues while masking the attack from the comprehension of the general public. For to openly besmirch a fellow professional is, first, unethical and anti-Hippocratic, and second, leaves a bad blot on the professional escutcheon. Of all the branches of psychiatric and social therapy which are being practiced today, psychoanalysis finds itself most open to criticism. For that reason, members of the Old Guard must take special care not to throw stones in their own glass houses. At times, then, when T-1 wishes to smudge T-2 a bit, he uses the word *Unconventional*.

To the laymen, *Unconventional* means "receptive to new ideas, willing to try new things." To the professional, it means "poorly disciplined, prone to *act-out*." The following table illustrates other words which can be used negatively by T-1, while at the same time he retains the respect, even admiration, on the part of laymen for professionals and the field as a whole:

Word Applied to T-2	Laymen's Interpretation	Therapists' Interpretations
a. Unorthodox	Flexible, interesting, pioneerlike	Poorly trained, quixotic, unreliable
b. Sweet	Sympathetic, kind	Incompletely analyzed, incapable of dealing with aggression, open to countertransference
c. Workmanlike, well-adjusted	Strong, reliable	Insensitive to emotional nuance
d. Primarily a Theoretician	Intellectually gifted	Ineffective with "real problems"
e. Good Guy	Pleasant	Schlemiel-like

played to prove ST's superiority. Often the ST, weighted as he is in private practice, not having published as much as he would like to, welcomes an opportunity to be revered by his Cs in a teaching capacity.

1. *Let Me Tell You How I'd Have Done It*

This is a rather simple game, consisting of the following ploys:

   a. ST listens without comment as C presents his case. (Time elapsed: twenty minutes)
   b. When C has finished, ST says, *"Let me tell you how I'd have done it . . ."* (Time elapsed: three seconds)
   c. ST embarks on a nonstop flight of explanation, expounding the nature of the case and all its possible interpretations. (Time elapsed: an hour and ten minutes)

ST's hope is that all Cs present will marvel at his intelligence and acuity. Certainly he himself is impressed, judging by the length of his production. The fact that *Let Me Tell You How I'd Have Done It* prevents the give-and-take of a good discussion (offering instead C's monologue [a], followed by ST's monologue [c]) means that ST is spared exposure as an ordinary thinker. The pay-off consists in the sight of C, and his fellow students, wide-eyed and hanging on every word. The let-down occurs on noting stifled yawns and glazed eyes.

2. *Ask Me a Question*

Here ST, faced with a class of Cs, wishes to be seen as an omniscient being, much as the Answer Man who led a popular radio show some years ago.

Ask Me a Question consists in ST's report of a case followed by an invitation to Cs to ask him relevant questions concerning material and method of treatment. To bring the game off successfully, ST need only have:

a. an illustration from one of those rare situations in which ST's words have a dramatic and positive effect on P
b. preplanned answers
c. novitiate Cs who are naïve enough to ask only those questions the answers for which are already implied in the report

There is, actually, no question which can be asked which cannot be answered adequately in therapeutic lingo. For example:

C-1: You said the patient had a compulsive need to drink milkshakes in spite of a weight problem, and that you interpreted this to mean the presence of a mother fixation. Why?

ST: Unsatisfactory breastfeeding in infancy.

C-2: You also mentioned that the milkshakes were always chocolate. What importance did that have?

ST: Compulsive toilet-training on the part of the mother, leading to preoccupation with feces.

C-3: What about the fact that the patient used spoons instead of straws?

ST: Fear of phallic symbols as competitive with mother's domination.

C-4: (brightly) And the fact that following your interpretation the patient went on a diet and took up smoking—this was based on a need for oral satisfaction to make up for the absence of the milkshakes?

ST: No, not at all. In giving up the milkshakes, *i.e.,* rejection of mother, and moving toward the father through the use of cigarettes, *i.e.,* phallic symbols,

guilt arose, demanding masochism through the
harmful use of self, *i.e.,* smoking.

3. *So What Do You Think It Was All About?*

In this game, ST exacts proper and precise information
from C. C, quite brilliantly, sums up a case in detail and
comes to the correct conclusion. He could not, were he himself an ST, have been more basic or all-inclusive. ST, in turn,
suggests, in effect, that C *Dig Deeper:*

> C: . . . and I conclude, therefore, that all emotional
> phenomena resulting in fear of darkness were due
> to P's unconscious knowledge that his mother did
> not welcome the pregnancy and wished to kill the
> fetus while it was still in the womb . . . Had P's
> father welcomed his birth, the trauma might well
> have been mitigated to a degree. But in fact P's
> father was in no mood for it, having at that time
> been "blackballed," to use the P's own phrase, by
> the country club in which he wished to acquire mem-
> bership. Here I saw the double-rejection, so to speak,
> compounded by the word "black" as it relates to
> "darkness."

> ST: *So what do you think it was all about . . . ?*

Or

> C: . . . the young man in treatment was unduly self-
> effacing with other males and critical of every wom-
> an he had ever known. One day he reported a dream
> in which he attended a classroom of some sort in
> which there was a discussion of Greek drama. I sug-
> gested to him that, in the dream, he was in truth
> discussing the Greek drama of *Oedipus Rex;* that if
> he could see it in this light, the dream would clarify
> his relationship with men and women alike, namely,
> point up the fact that his attitudes toward them
> served to *deny* his wish to have intercourse with his

mother and slay his father Following my interpretation, he became bolder in therapy, more direct with men, fonder of women, and is now engaged to be married.

ST: *So what do you think it was all about . . . ?*

4. Mama or Papa

Since no human being, born in or out of wedlock, is without mother *and* father, conflicts arising in children are influenced by both. In the physical absence of one or both parents, there are influences which may in fact be as important as, if not more important than, the influences of those who remain present. "Marriage," whether legal or not, is a relationship in which both members participate constantly in that each plays an emotional role for the other. Where mother is dominant, father must be weaker; where father is strong, mother is submissive. This interaction of personalities continues throughout time, shedding its shower of stars upon the heads of all offspring. It is impossible, then, to analyze the responses of any human being in terms of one parent to the total exclusion of the other. Oedipus, so tragically involved with his mother, was indeed as involved with the father whom he slew.

Because of the back-and-forth swap of neurosis origins, ST, dealing with C's attempt at interpretation, can choose as he wishes:

C: In this case, the girl I've been treating is decidedly fixated on father. To begin with, he wanted a male child. So he had her wearing pants and swinging baseball bats from the time she was five. From this came her identification with the male figure which later resulted in her homosexuality. I've spent six months with her and I've come to the definite conclusion that it's Papa . . .

ST: It's Mama.

Or

C: In this case, the girl I've been treating is decidedly fixated on mother. To begin with, mother wanted a female child. So she overprotected the girl and taught her to be afraid of boys from the time she was five. From this came the girl's enslavement to the female figure which later resulted in her homosexuality. I've spent six months with her, and I've come to the definite conclusion that it's Mama.

ST: It's Papa.

5. *Transference* (*replay*)

To repeat, transference is a term used to describe certain patterns of behavior shown by P toward significant people in his past (*i.e.*, his mother and father) which he then "transfers" to T.

In the game of *Transference* as played with Cs, ST shows his acuteness publicly by using a variation of *Mama or Papa*. When C reports transference material which has arisen in his case with P, ST need only ask: "Whom do you think P sees you as—the mother or the father?"

The game quality of *Transference* (as opposed to its true value when used legitimately) becomes evident when one realizes that:

a. ST asks C the question at relatively irrelevant times, *i.e.*, while C's P is trying to cope with the death of a husband, is getting out of a bad marriage, or is panicked with guilt over a recent abortion, or

b. when the clinical data is insufficient to provide C with a reasonably certain answer.

The second situation is the best in which to play the game because C, rather than admit ignorance, feels obliged to answer, and when he does, ST suggests that the transference lies with the other parent.

6. *Countertransference* (*replay*)

Used accusatorially throughout all gamey therapeutic relationships, *Countertransference* is, again, one of the simplest ploys in dampening C's self-ardor to the enhancement of ST's superiority. Where C, not fully educated, still in his larval state, cannot see the insidious tentacles of his own subjectivity, ST is quick to point them out:

C: I would like to speak of a new development in the case I reported last week—the girl who is training to become an international spy.

ST: Isn't it odd that you speak of this particular case to the exclusion of all others, week after week after week?

C: Well, I just wanted to say that I have made a connection between her choice of profession and her unresolved conflicts centering about the Primal Scene.

ST: What are your personal feelings about this patient?

C: (pausing) I find her . . . well, her verbal productions are interesting.

ST: Countertransference.

E. Superannuation Games

Just as the number-one child tells his siblings, "I'm right because I'm older than you!"—so does the age and past experience of a supperannuated T bring with it a nobility and a glory of its own.

At any social or professional gathering, the presence of a member of the Old Guard presents a certain aura which evokes, at best, respect and a quiet awe; at worst, fawning.

We are, today, running low on these adulated creatures. In 1969 there are not many American Ts left who have actually studied with or been analyzed by Sigmund Freud, Eugen Bleuler, Josef Breuer, Sandor Ferenczi, or even Ernest Jones.

Superannuated Ts are well aware of the position they hold, and they make the most of it. The following game is played by Ts of sixty-five years or older whose professional careers are virtually behind them. They are steeped in nostalgic remembrances of things past.

1. *Celebrity*

Of all superannuation games, *Celebrity* is by far the best:

In his youth, Dr. Finstermacher had been in the forefront of the psychoanalytic movement. He received his own analysis from the Master himself, wrote and published prolifically and was subsequently quoted by two generations of younger therapists.

Now in his seventy-eighth year, he is semiretired, seeing just those few Ps whom he has not been able to terminate. His hearing is poor; his eyesight is failing. He has not published anything for the past fifteen years, and has failed to keep abreast of the latest analytic thinking for the past four. Nonetheless, his name is forever enshrined in the history of the Movement, and his books grace any decent therapeutic library.

Such was his reputation that even today, in his senescence, he is frequently called upon to address large public audiences and student-groups, for the "charisma" of his name is sure to fill and overfill any conference room or auditorium. On these occasions, those assembled witness a frail man, led haltingly to the podium, shawl draped about stooped shoulders, who recounts in a faltering voice folksy but awe-striking anecdotes in the lives of the immortals:

1. I recall the evening when Jung and I were scheduled to speak before a large group, such as this one, and . . .
2. . . . so after I finished describing this dream to Freud, he said to me, "Well, Finstermacher, I'll be frank with you . . ."
3. Erich was always a difficult person to work with. I remember once when he came to me about a problem he was having with a particular patient, and I said . . .
4. Anna had this funny habit at parties of always . . .

5. It's hard to believe, but it seemed to me that Ernest was always overcompensating for a writer's block . . .
6. It was I who first told Wilhelm Reich, "Watch it, boy . . . you're going off the track."
7. It might be said that while the rest of us were reading Theodor Reik's first book, I was listening to him with my "third ear" . . .

If *Celebrity* is played by a septuagenarian who was just an ordinary T in his youth, he can substitute place-dropping for name-dropping, contenting himself with memories of the towns, conferences, and institutions which were at one time frequented by giants:

1. When I was in Zurich . . .
2. One day in Freiberg, Austria, which is now Pvibor, Czechoslovakia . . .
3. Once, in a class at the Leopoldstader Kommunareal and Obergymnasium, which acquired the colloquial name of Sperlgymnasium after 1870 when it expanded from the Taborgasse into the Sperlgasse . . .

When several Old Guard Ts meet socially, the game becomes more competitive:

OGT-1: I remember a patient I had who, following analysis, became a well-known radio-announcer.
OGT-2: I remember one from a more recent year who, following treatment, went on to become a prominent television personality.
OGT-3: That reminds me of a patient of mine who, following a bad case of agoraphobia, actually became a stage-and-screen idol.
OGT-4: I found the theatrical personality rather shallow in terms of case-interest. I do recall, however, a young politician who abhorred public speaking, but who, following therapy, was elected President of the United States.

F. Podium-and-Paper Games

Therapeutic papers, or theses, before (hopefully) they are published, are often read at conventions or group meetings of T's particular institute. Ts of note are also invited to speak, for a fee, at public auditoriums, various Ys, and other gatherings to which laymen are invited. While some Ts are reticent, even fearful, of public speaking, most are touched with a bit of the Ham and revel in this form of exhibitionism. The podium symbolizes a kind of throne from which, usually standing, the king noblesse obliges down into a sea of eager and rapt faces.

There are, on the whole, five major types of oral offerings as exemplified by the following topics:

1. *The Contribution of Dr. Freihoffer*
2. *Depression as a Manifestation of Depression*
3. *Homosexuality as Influenced by Archaic Super-Ego Introjects*
4. *The Relationship of Eye Movements in Sleeping Fish to Castration Dreams in Six-Month-Old Males: Its Implications for Further Research in Ego Development*
5. *The Mass-Appeal Mother-Surrogate: A Comparative Study of Gertrude Berg, Marlene Dietrich, and Carol Burnett*

In the presentation of (1), Dr. Freihoffer himself has just delivered a paper before the American Society of Psychoanalytic Therapists—perhaps on the subject of (4).

Dr. Breslo is the first person scheduled to discuss the paper. He has been given an advance copy the week before, by the Director of the Society, and, try as he did, he has been unable to palm the assignment off on anyone else. Resenting the task and never able to suffer fools gladly, he has still made a stab at comprehending Dr. Freihoffer's theory, and is prepared to praise the lecture, adding, of course, his own tidbits of originality.

"It has been said of Dr. Freihoffer, known as Fish-Fry to his more intimate friends, that when it comes to the Unconscious, he can stay under longer than anybody . . ."

There is a ripple of appreciative laughter which will, in fact, be the last ripple of the evening.

When, finally, the *Contribution of Dr. Freihoffer* has been sufficiently examined and analyzed, Dr. Breslo adds at least one of his own perceptions:

"While it is difficult to supplement Freihoffer's theories— so thorough are they in concept and development—it occurs to me to suggest to you the relationship between fish and male masturbation. In closing, I leave you with this thought: *The fish is a phallic symbol.* Thank you."

In the presentation of (2), Dr. Clapp has been asked to deliver his own paper, based on four years of research at one of the local universities. The subject is Depression. When, an hour later, he has explored all causes and effects, which may or may not be due to "unrealistic overprotection by Mother in childhood," he winds up with the theory that depression is brought on by unhappiness.

In the presentation of topic (3), Dr. Margolis plays the game of *Big Words (and Bigger* Words) and translates a commonly accepted theory into language which will impress his listeners. We know that homosexuality is rarely "constitutional," or based in organic origins, and that it is caused by various interrelationships in childhood with mother and father. To refer to mother and father as *archaic super-ego introjects* is to add the essential fillip.

In the presentation of (4), Dr. Freihoffer offers a theory which involves both zoology and medicine. Rare is the T who remembers what he learned at medical school. The medical prerequisite for psychoanalysts has in fact been frequently questioned. Ps reporting severe headaches or other physical symptomology might just as easily be referred to straight

MDs or Internists. Yet Ts prefer to interpret all physical phenomena in terms of emotional origins—as in the case of George Gershwin.

Be that as it may, Dr. Freihoffer's retention of his early training is indeed impressive. It can be assumed that he is not one for treating brain cancer as a form of mother-fixation.

For the presentation of his Paper (5), Dr. Carter faces a mixed audience of professionals and laymen at the YMCA. He wishes to appeal not only to his colleagues, but also to the general public. Therefore, his contribution is based securely in therapeutic data, but at the same time allows the common man to "identify." The topic, then, must be chosen for its basis in ordinary life. What better than a comparative study of three figures from the world of stage, screen, and television who have been viewed by millions? Dr. Carter has already read the actual paper of William Park based on the relation of Doris Day to the Madonna, and he knows its attractions. This evening, he will triple the impact: Gertrude Berg was, after all, the prototype of the Jewish Mother. Marlene Dietrich is the mother who might well have been fantasied by Alex Portnoy. And Carol Burnett is important in that, confronted by her as a maternal object, one might prefer Alex Portnoy's *real* mother.

It should be noted, however, that while Dr. Carter's paper is met with enthusiastic applause, he is playing a dangerous game. Ts who are too easily understood and appreciated by laymen fall into disrepute among their peers. It has been said of Edmund Bergler, whose books often approached best-sellerdom, that he was a "sensationalist"—albeit a rich one; and of Helene Deutsch that she "wrote too well to be trustworthy."

Freud himself was a writer of clarity and wit, but what is accepted from him shall not be forgiven in his disciples.

XV. Games Played Socially

At a party, a well-known T got up from his chair, sat down at the piano, and burst into a medley of tinkling numbers. Said he, with a broad grin, "Let's give 'em a look at the Analyst at Play!"

While the manifest content of this remark proved his desire to display his "humanness," its latent content indicates the self-consciousness of a basic belief in superiority.

The host and hostess (H and HS) whose party list includes analysts, artists, and other guests of interest (G), are presumably sophisticated enough, as are their Gs, to take all professionals with a modicum of equanimity, if not a grain of salt. There is, in reality, little awesomeness in such groups. For one thing, H, HS, and G all have probably been analyzed to one degree or another and have observed the wide range of T's games. Also, they are relatively secure.

Yet the T, steeped as he is in the aura created about him in the American Twentieth Century, continues to think of himself as special. Try as he may, he is unable to join any group of human beings with a complete acceptance of the fact that he is "just another guest" who will *not* be expected to sing (or play) for his supper.

Unlike the others who walk with balanced gait, T's best foot is forever being put forward. In fantasy, and often in fact, he has a kind of personal pipeline to the residual problems of all those present, and can, with ease, spot their hidden motivations. In most cases this "talent" is based on his training. What he fails to recognize is the fact that those around him, untrained, are often blessed with an innate

T: Oh, forty-one, forty-two.

G: That's too young. Must be situational. Brought on by some unexpected trauma?

T: Well, it seems there's trouble with his father in their business. They own a Ford agency, matter of fact. Down on Broad Street. I can't tell you the name, of course. But suffice it to say the owners sold the building and they've got to move. It's a Strauss-Greenberg building, and they're renting to Penn Fruit. The result is, this patient of mine can't get it up. Wife came to see me last week, says she's tried everything and is considering divorce. What a job I got, I tell *you,* there are days when I wish I'd stuck to straight medicine . . .

T has now impressed G with his professional trials and tribulations. He has also given out P's identity. Ford dealerships, as with all automobile agencies, are spaced geographically to avoid cutthroat competition within any single neighborhood. Anyone who has driven into town, or who knows the city at all, is aware that the Ford agency on Broad Street is called Bernstein Ford, Inc. Another automobile dealer, standing a few feet away from this verbal exchange, knows that the P in question is Harry Bernstein's son, George. It is also known among several other Gs that Strauss-Greenberg has a sign outside of Bernstein's announcing the subsequent arrival of a new Penn Fruit store. George's problem will now become an intriguing grape on the suburban and center-city vine. But T has succeeded in holding the interest of his audience without so much as mentioning P's or P's father's actual name.

B. It's Your Narcissism

Most Gs have the courtesy to refrain from asking personal questions of professionals at a social gathering. Hardly anyone would consider, for example, buttonholing a lawyer and asking him, between the main course and dessert, for advice on how to handle an accident case or a deadbeat customer. Yet this courtesy is not always retained in the case of therapists. Small talk at parties is essential, and Gs know that Ts take pleasure in small talk which relates to their work. The work is, after all, based in human relationship, calling for a certain brilliance and acuity on the part of those who are in charge.

In this example, G can't think of anything to say to T, so she throws out a casual observation of Self. She tells him, amicably, that she is pleased to discover that since she has begun to smoke again, she has been able to adhere more firmly to her diet. She has, in fact, been successful enough to join Weight Watchers, and within six months she will be the sylph she was at nineteen.

The game-free T will recognize this as a pleasant piece of news, to be greeted with a simple, "That's great! I saw how beautiful you looked the minute I walked in!" Following this, G will find herself happy and filled with self-esteem, feelings which would normally allow her to move on to other Gs at the party and have a good time.

The T, however, who cannot for a minute "forget himself" will answer, "Hhmmnn. What this means . . . is that, uh, you're need for oral satisfaction has, uh . . . yielded to your wish to be attractive. In other words, um . . . *it's your narcissism* . . ."

A well-egofied G will respond with, "Up yours." The less bold G will end up with the wind knocked out of her sails. *Narcissism?* Is that *good . . . ?* May it not suggest that there are still other unresolved conflicts? And what about the normal need for oral satisfaction? *Should* this be repressed in favor of self-love? And is not oral satisfaction in fact a form of self-love?

Meanwhile, T has scored. Friendly, but not warm; understanding, but not compassionate; funny, but not witty; educated, but not intuitive; wishing for lightness, but inescapably heavy—he has made his presence known.

C. Give Me a Call and We'll See

Every so often a T at a party will, through practice, give off the impression that he is in truth a *Great Guy*. Having worked with Ps since 8:00 A.M. that morning (and on Saturday, when other professionals and business owners stay at home and relax, or join their wives and children in some special expedition), T arrives at the home of his H and HS in fine fettle. Tired, yes, but maintaining still the openly social front; up to the ears in people and people's problems, but not so deeply spent that he cannot meet with more of them.

With the seemingly casual air of an ordinary and loving comrade, he throws his arm across G-1's shoulders. "How's it going, man? Life treating you okay?" For G-2, clacking ice cubes against the sides of her empty glass, he goes into the next room and brings her a refill. To G-3, a Las Vegas buff, he offers to drop off an interesting book by John Scarne the next time he happens to be in the neighborhood. With G-4, he shares the fond memory of a joint hunting trip several years back when T thought for one fleeting second that his friend's red cap was part of the shrubbery. And for G-5, well known for her reticence and manifestations of depression, he leaves less amusing Gs in order to sit by her side and engage her in conversation. She is, by nature, and psychical bent, difficult to talk with. Her antisocialness (based on fear, not aloofness) compels her to be almost monosyllabic. She is mistress of the one-word answer:

T: (offering her a cigarette which she rejects) So what's new? Haven't seen you around for a while.

G: No.

T: Jim and the kids okay?

G: Okay.

T: Happened to run into Jim a couple weeks ago on the street. He tell you?

G: No.

T: Gave me great reports on you. Said you were taking up your music again, doing scales all night.

G: Yes.

T: Enjoying it?

G: It's all right.

T: I had a patient once, musically inclined like you are. It's very special, music is. I mean most of the people artistically inclined, that is—painters and the like— they're visual. You can't see music. You can see the notes, I don't mean that—I mean the finished product, the performance, so to speak, isn't visual. It's aural.

G: Yes.

T: This patient of mine, she was a woman, too, in the course of the analysis it occurred to me, the Visual vs. the Aural Personality. Matter of fact, I wrote a paper on it.

G: Oh.

T: Very interesting. Do you find by any chance that even though you think you want to play the piano, you get up after a few minutes, a half hour or so, and you're a little depressed?

G: Sometimes.

T: Ah. Well, you've had therapy, haven't you?

G: Only two years.

T: Hhmmnn. Well, did you ever get to it? I mean that depression you feel after playing the piano? Did you gain any insight?

G: Not that I know of.

T: I had this idea, I got it while I was working with this

other patient I mentioned, that the Aural orientation, so to speak, might be a denial of some archaic Visuality. By that I mean to say, something was "seen" in childhood which brought with it a sense of guilt or self-recrimination. You know what I mean?

G: No.

T: Primal Scene.

G: Oh.

T: (leaning forward solicitously) Pretty simple, you know. Person with your sensitivity, you should be able to work out that little kink in no time at all.

G: (sufficiently interested to be aroused) You mean I could enjoy it more, I could improve in my technique, if I—

T: Absolutely.

G: How?

T: (having gone far enough) *Give me a call,* why don't you, and *we'll see* . . .

   T is, after all, a professional. While he is willing to strew a bit of largess about for free, he is too aware of his position and the impression he makes upon the layman to give it *all* away. G may or may not bother to call; in many instances, she does, even though it may be several months or a year later.

D. Oedipal Conflict (replay)

Oedipal Conflict, when played socially, is a whisper-behind-the-hand game. It is one of the most irritating tricks in T's social bag because it accomplishes two questionable ends:

1. It forces H, HS, or G into the role of accomplice; and
2. people sense when they are being talked about, so that

the G who is the subject of T's whispering is often aware that he is that subject and is either embarrassed or rendered paranoid. (In this case, however, he only feels that way. There is some question as to whether one can be labeled "paranoid" when he is aware that someone actually *is* "persecuting" him.)

For example: G-1 is engaged in conversation with G-2 and G-3.

G-1: . . . so I asked her to please stay a half hour overtime and finish up the mail, and she told me she was too tired, besides which she had a dinner date at seven.

G-2: It's hard to keep secretaries these days. I usually avoid the problem by dictating early in the morning, so by five-thirty she's through anyway.

G-3: It's difficult when they've got dinner dates. I mean you can't expect them to give their entire lives up for the damned job.

G-1: This is not a "damned job." She's been raised three times this year, and pretty soon she'll be making more than I do. When I ask a woman to do something for me once in a while, and I'm paying her, I expect her to do it.

G-2: Well, she's got other interests . . .

G-1: Other interests? You should see the jerk she's been dating. Hangs around the office an hour before she's ready to go. A real wash-out, believe me. She winds him around her little finger . . . It would be worth it to me to fire *her,* just to get rid of *him.*

At this point, T leans toward H, HS, or G-4, and behind his hand, all-knowing gleam in his eye, whispers just loud enough to be heard by everyone: "Oedipal Conflict . . ."

The point of the game is to impress H, HS, and G-4 with the fact that T is more perceptive than they are; and to establish himself as a contributing member of the gathering.

Depending upon the material of the conversation between Gs which is being overheard, *Oedipal Conflict* becomes interchangeable with:

1. *Latent Homosexuality*
2. *Penis Envy*
3. *Mother Fixation*
4. *Father Fixation*
5. *Narcissism*
6. *Manic-Depressiveness*
7. *Countertransference*

and countless numbers of other one-word, or one-phrase, labels applied, completely out of context with the basic personality, to any individual who expresses any passing thought in any manner.

E. Great-Grandmother

Great-Grandmother is yet another way for T to display brilliance in a social milieu. As we have already pointed out, most of the parties to which T is invited are made up of people who are reasonably sophisticated. The majority of them have experienced some form of therapy; those who have not, have been exposed to at least some psychiatric literature. Because of this, simple, all-inclusive labels, such as listed in *Oedipal Conflict,* are used as glibly by Gs as they are by Ts. In this day and age the mystery of Oedipus Rex, for example, has lost its previous esoteric and cultural aura. *Oedipal Conflict* and *Oedipal Triangle* are household phrases.

Even those who do not use the terminology are aware of its implications, as is proven by the popularity of the joke in which a relatively uneducated mother says of her son, "Isn't he wonderful! He goes to a psychiatrist, lies down on a couch, pays thirty-five dollars an hour—and who do you think he talks about? ME!"

In view of the mass usage of so many therapeutic words and concepts, it falls upon T to complicate matters a bit. To know something which is already known by everyone else is to stoop to equality; and since equality with laymen is, for T, a kind of inferiority, he must prove that there are secrets which no one else has even dreamed of.

In the social discussion of any case, the P may sooner or later be evaluated as a victim of some sort of Oedipal problem. Whether he sucks his thumb at the age of forty-seven, wets his bed at thirty-six, or falls prey to sexual fantasies involving necrophilia, we can be sure that the root of the trouble lies with *Mama or Papa.*

In order to prevent Gs from jumping the gun on him, T plays *Great-Grandmother.* In reporting the case to goggle-eyed listeners, he points out the crucial importance in the life of P of the least likely person imaginable—such as the great-grandmother who died the week P was born, a second cousin who lived in a distant city and was seen only twice by P in his entire thirty-five or forty years, or a substitute-teacher in P's third-grade of elementary school, who taught P's class for three consecutive days in the winter of 1937.

The game of *Great-Grandmother,* or its variations, has both active and passive versions:

1. Active

T describes a fascinating case about a young man who was, for years, sexually aroused by high-button shoes. Three previous Ts, he discloses, proved incapable of helping the poor chap. T, on the other hand, cured him within two months after directing him to associate to his *great-grandmother.*

2. Passive:

T listens to G who is sociably describing the case of a brother-in-law who has developed a unique tic: He tightens his lips, forces air between them, and gives forth with something resembling the Bronx Cheer. Other Gs in the group offer the obvious interpretations, involving mother, father, siblings, early lovers.

T, playing it passively, offers no corrections, makes no statements. Instead, he asks a question: "Have you thought of the possibility that it is related to his aunt-by-marriage who may have lived on the Concourse?"

Another G tells the story of a girl she knew at college who went on safari and reached orgasm when she was bitten by an alligator. His fellow-G offers the interpretation that alligators, which are reptiles, are also phallic symbols: ergo, the phenomenon related to Father.

T steps in at the appropriate moment and asks: "Did she by any chance, in early childhood, live next to a pet shop?"

The passive version of *Great-Grandmother* (2) is the more popular for its subtlety. Also, it harks back to various games played with T by his training analyst and his supervisor—*i.e.,* the questions asked of T, who was then C, in Chapter 2.

F.   We

The Editorial *We* is irritating even when it is used by a single individual who is indeed writing or speaking editorially. It is far more forceful to use *I*. It is also less safe.

T, challenged by Gs to explain some strange or incredible

concept or therapeutic policy, plays the *We* game almost automatically. Thrown, for the evening, among laymen, a stranger mid alien corn, he bolsters his courage by calling into play the entire cast of thousands who belong to his own particular institute:

> G: Don't you think that loss of memory can sometimes be caused by brain damage or some other organic defect, and that it needn't always be a matter of one's *wanting* to forget?
>
> T: Well, *we* believe . . .

G. They

They is the word used to refer to any member of the therapeutic world who is *not* a member of T's own particular institute. This is, for example, true in Philadelphia, where the Psychoanalytic Institute and the Psychoanalytic Association form two separate groups, both working simultaneously. Similar situations exist in New York, Washington, D.C., and other large cities.

When G asks T, who happens to be a member of the Association, "How come it takes you so long to analyze a patient when the Institute boys do it about two years faster?" T is apt to say, "Well, *they* think . . .," the emphasis on *they* somehow implying that *they* don't know what *they're* doing.

H. Ho Ho

Ho Ho is another game which T plays when he is either listening directly to, or eavesdropping on, the lay-Gs who surround him. A better game than *It's Your Narcissism, Oedipal Conflict,* and *Great-Grandmother,* it fills several bills at once:

1. It assures T of G's respect.

2. It sets the wheels of mystery in motion without ever producing a direct or definite explanation.
3. It saves T the trouble of working overtime, at least in the verbal sense.
4. It keeps T from getting into an intellectual spot.
5. It fits into any and all situations.

Examples:

1. G: What do you think of Edward Albee?
   T: *Ho ho* . . .

2. G-1: It may snow again.
   G-2: Damn it, I hate winter.
   T: *Ho ho* . . .

3. G-3: (female) Gosh, it's hard handling this lasagna.
   G-4: (male) Here—use my knife.
   T: Ho . . . *ho!*

5. G-7: (female) That same magazine salesman keeps coming back at the most inconvenient times.
   G-8: (female) I don't answer the door for strange men; you never know what can happen.
   T: *Hoooo!*

6. G-9: (female) How are you?
   G-10: (female) Not so hot. My period is late again.
   T: Ho *ho* ho . . .

Ho Ho is, in reality, a substitute for the child's taunt: "I know something *yooooou* don't know!" Whether T does is sometimes questionable, but the game is a star *shtick* for the getting of attention. In these fleeting exchanges between Gs, it would be overshooting the mark to plaster the *Oedipal Conflict* banner across G's psyche. If T is too obvious in his approach to social behavior (his own), he is likely, at some point or other, to be gibed in return by a brave and heedless

G—or even worse, by that bane of his existence: the lowly Social Worker.

Ho Ho is safer. At worst, T may be accused of a Santa Claus Identification.

Special note should be made of the social behavior of female analysts. It is, if anything, played down. While the male T is free to assume his role of professional in the world, while professionality is in fact expected of him, the female T in America is up against the same problems as her nonpro, housewife-type counterparts. Back in the suffragette days, the winning of the vote was an empty symbol. Never in Freud's life did he ever achieve total adjustment to the equality of women with men. The product of the Victorian Age, furthermore the son of a domineering mother, he found all signs of intelligence and material success in women to be due to masculine traits. And as Freud goes, so goes the country. European women who have reached their goals by way of intellect, insight, and a certain healthy aggressivity are accepted as part of the natural order of things. Anna Freud, for example, is admired for her brilliance in the psychotherapeutic field. Here, her success would be related to a Father Identification. Freud himself often referred to her as "my favorite son."

The female T in America is wholly conscious of our Battle of the Sexes. She knows well that it is a battle which, if she is to retain her womanhood, she must lose.

Her social behavior, then, is attuned to this concept. She dresses attractively, makes much of emptying ashtrays, neatening tables, and seeing that the people around her are comfortable. Often, when she has piled her plate high with buffet food, she offers it to someone else, preferring to wait another turn. For woman is not Woman unless she is also Mother.

When asked socially for professional advice, she is apt to change the subject or to smile graciously and say, "Come on now, we're here to have fun" or, "You know . . . I hadn't quite thought about it . . ." Instead of displaying her knowledge of the field, she will speak charmingly about her children, report the redecorating of her living room, stick close to the side of her husband.

She is not entirely pleased when she is described as "brilliant." She would much rather leave behind her the impression that she is "nice."

PART III

A Theory of Change

A Theory of Change

A complete disavowal of Freud would be both unintelligent and impossible. It is our feeling that far too much time and energy is spent in the therapeutic field trying to invalidate the experiments and findings of innovators rather than in trying to substantiate the valid aspects of innovation. For example: "The techniques of Dr. X show themselves to be beneficial for several years, after which period there is evidence of patient-relapse; taking the long-term view, the success or failure of his work just about parallels that of other psychiatrists using conventional methods." We suggest a more profitable critique, one which might have sought to point out those aspects of Dr. X's technique which were "beneficial for several years."

Similarly, we are less concerned with establishing an elaborate theory of change than we are with suggesting *particular* changes in the style of classical therapists which will, in turn, promote a more rapid resolution in the life style of classical patients. In truth, we are more interested in deeds than in words.

Freud's contributions must be viewed from both theoretical and practical standpoints. Our criticism of classical Freudian technique is, then, one which seeks to expand the limited options which such a technique imposes on therapist and patient alike, and which unduly prolongs the process of treatment. But first, a run-down of Freud's important contributions is in order:

1. He destroyed the notion that the intellect reigned su-

preme, and demonstrated that human beings are moved by forces within their psychical and emotional makeups—forces which usually exist *outside of awareness* or, as he called it, in the Unconscious Mind.

2. He pointed out that the emotions which gave the greatest trouble to the greatest number of people were those involving sex and aggression.

3. While Aristotle wrote that a man's true life is lived in his dreams, it was Freud who formulated the theory and put it to active use. Dreams were, as he put it, "the royal road to the Unconscious." Used in therapy, they afforded important means of making people aware of their heretofore unnoticed attitudes and feelings.

4. He was the formulator of the *lapsus linguae* (slip-of-the-tongue) concept, a theoretical phenomenon closely related to free association; if a patient is encouraged to say everything which comes into his mind without previous thought, without the controlling and censorious elements of self-approval or disapproval, he will eventually reach the rock-bottom of his hidden attitudes, gain insight into himself, and ultimately be able to discard his neurotic behavior patterns.

5. It was Freud's belief that the child's earliest training and environmental factors have profound influence on his later attitudes toward life. In other words: *As the twig is bent, so grows the tree.*

Freud's methods were, undoubtedly, the best available at the time. On the other hand, we find fault with those of his followers who stop cold at this point, and who fail to take advantage of the building, or psychosynthetic, *growth*-assisting processes, who rely solely on the psychoanalytic aspects of treatment. Also we find fault with any theory which purports to explain all data by elevating one concept, at the expense of any other, to a position of primacy. An important example is the Oedipus Theory. The Oedipus Complex is, in essence, only a symbol. While it is quite true that most human interactions can be reduced to Oedipal symbology, they can also be reduced to questions of life and death, passivity and aggressivity, good and evil, outer-and-inner-directedness, heat and cold, right and wrong, yin and yang, and so forth. Indeed, the story of Oedipus Rex can be broken down into any or all of these polarities—including Sophocles' own belief that tragedy lay in the hands of the gods.

Here again, it serves well to point out the highly personalized and deeply subjective origins from which most of our accepted theoretical concepts have stemmed:

Freud was cursed (if undeniably blessed as well) with a doting, devoted, and domineering mother to whom "mein goldene Siggie" was the most important and beloved member of the family. Quite naturally he employed this factor in his evolution of a theory based on the Sophoclean tragedy of a young man named Oedipus who killed his father and married his mother—an action which led to inevitable and unmitigated doom.

Sullivan grew up in a rural wilderness. For the most part, he related to animals. Given this deprivation, it followed that he should develop a theory of psychology based on the importance of interpersonal relationships.

Adler, a man of frail physique, placed great emphasis on body defects as a source of neurosis, and brought forth a theory of Inferiority *vs.* Superiority.

Horney, a woman, thought in terms of cycles.

Melanie Klein, also a woman, wrote extensively about intrauterine experience, and established a theory based on breast-feeding: to eat and be eaten.

Jung, an Aryan who later argued in favor of Hitler's ideas of racial superiority, formulated a concept of the *racial,* or collective, *unconscious,* thus taking a bit of the heat off the individual and placing it in a context of mythology and the past history of entire societies.

Szasz, by nature a nonconformist, comes out strongly against the categorization and labeling of mental disease *as* disease, and has had enormous success with schizophrenics whom he finds to be simply less-conforming types of human beings.

In view of these concepts and their personally based roots, it is difficult to ascribe to any in particular the rating of one-and-only. Which, if any, is the Real Thing? And what sense does it make to live and practice by a single theory?

Our argument, then, is not against variations in ideology, but with techniques of operation. Whether the therapist is Freudian, Jungian, or Horneyan, he will, if he is a classical technician, direct his patient to "discover" all, while "doing" nothing. For example, the Freudian analyst, confronted with a patient suffering from feelings of persecution, will take him back to the influences of his childhood: the entanglement with mother and father. A Jungian treating that same patient might go beyond individual background into the realms of an historical persecution. Otto Rank specialized in the creative personality, which he found to be quite differently motivated from others; his focal point, again in relation to the same patient, might be the stresses and strains of art.

In all three examples, the push would be for analysis-cum-insight, rather than for doing and learning through alterations in active living.

We believe that the process of living involves continuous changes in perspective. Further, we believe in teaching patients to think for themselves, much as the great therapists of history thought, felt, and acted for themselves. People must be opened up to the richness which exists in the ever-shifting sands of ideology and experience. To insist that they reduce all material to one final concept is not teaching them how to live. These victims of dogmatic technique and theorization are being taught not to think and evaluate, but to worship. Granted the Oedipal Triangle problem exists, to one degree or another, in all of us; granted, it was the key issue in Freud's personal life; this, however, does not necessarily make it a universal key issue.

How, then, to bring about change?

To reiterate in some measure:

A person goes to see a therapist because his life is not going the way he would like it to. He is not doing the things he would like to do, saying the things he would like to say, feeling the things he would like to feel. He is constrained or depressed, jealous or furious, hopeless or helpless. He is looking for a way out of this situation. He is counting on a change.

He finds it virtually impossible to change on his own. If he could, he would not become a patient. His ways of relating are quite limited. While he is able, often, to play one role well (be it that of the bully or the boy scout, the clown or the lost soul, the imbecile or the distraught genius, the moralist or the Don Juan, the intellectual, the martyr, the career girl, or the sexual tease), he cannot switch or combine roles—or maintain a psychological mobility which would afford him a far wider and more rewarding life experience.

He is also afraid to try to relate in new ways. This is unfamiliar ground; he has never learned how to cross it. His lack of self-confidence is alarming; he dreads attempting something at which he fears he might fail. He is cowed by the idea that any fumbling effort to relate in new ways will bring ridicule, shame, and guilt down upon his head. The result is that he dare not try, and remains trapped in his rut.

Believing that there is something shameful and peculiar about himself, he cannot permit himself to experience his full range of emotions. He is convinced that it is these very emotions which make him such an inferior character. And what he does experience of these emotions he is reluctant to share with others. His rage, therefore, or his lustfulness, his jealousies, envies, pettinesses, fears, ambitions, selfishness, or timidity become hidden.

Change is defined as "to become different, to vary, to enter upon a new phase." Insight is defined as "the ability of one who is mentally ill to recognize the nature of his disorder." How disappointing it will be if our therapeutic beginner falls into the hands of the "traditional" psychotherapist. For the traditionalist offers not change, but insight. He substitutes talk for action, intellectuality for experience. And many patients, lost and unsure of themselves, aware of the enormous body of psychoanalytic and psychotherapeutic literature on which ground-rules are based, awed by the respect which is given the psychotherapist in our culture, and hoping for a magical and effortless cure, will often spend months in treatment, if not years, before he recognizes the futility of such trials.

This emotional bankruptcy lies in the assumption that insight cures. More often than not the patient already "recognizes the nature of his disorder." He knows that his parents had certain destructive influences on him, appreciates his defensiveness, is aware that his neurotic terror of failure prevents him from going off in new directions. Much of what passes for therapeutic insight consists merely in translating the layman's terminology into Freudian language. But calling a running nose *rhinitis* does not really add much to one's knowledge. Similarly, calling the trap of mother-father confusion an *Oedipal Conflict* does not add a whit of understanding to the learning process.

When your car breaks down and you take it to a mechanic you do not want a dissertation on what made it develop mechanical trouble as much as you want him to take whatever action is needed to make the necessary repairs. By the same token, a young man, avoiding heterosexual experiences due to his past humiliations caused by impotence, will get little out of merely learning that this is related to a fear of being destroyed by a domineering mother. What is needed is something which goes beyond insight; something which will encourage him to reestablish contact with the opposite sex so that he may discover that there are women in this world who are not at all like his mother.

The courage needed to make such efforts is considerable. Many patients prefer to hope that their cures will result not from their actual efforts, but rather from merely discovering the causes of their difficulties, or from being offered some brilliant interpretation by their therapists. Unfortunately, the traditional therapist shares this illusion.

The reasons for this lie in the origins of the psychoanalytic movement where the nature of mental illnesses has been so extensively explored. While this exploration has revealed much about the workings of the mind, it has not necessarily shed light on the how-to aspect of disease-cure. Yet the nature of most therapeutic training (see Chapter 2) is so confused and disorganized, so heavily weighted in favor of genesis over cure, tradition over experimentation, that the practitioner can often lose track of what he actually is supposed to do.

If the therapist's role is not that of promotor-of-insight but rather catalyst-of-change, what are his means of bringing this about? We submit that he must use himself and his subjective reactions more openly and more fully, actively encourage adventurousness and experimentation in his patients, and be adept at verbal reconditioning.

Use of Therapeutic Subjectivity

As has been mentioned previously, there is much subjectivity which patients hide from themselves and others for fear that having certain reactions makes them subhuman. At the same time, therapists fear that having, and showing, certain reactions makes them subprofessional. The irony here is that it is only the open and fearless therapist who can act as a productive role-model for the uptight patient, thus displaying a pattern of real life behavior for the patient to follow. This therapist can rapidly accelerate the process of change.

Encouraging Adventurousness

The more one experiences, the richer life becomes. Indeed, life is change, is variability, is unpredictability and transformation. What is static and perpetually at rest is not living, but inorganic. There is so much in our lives which is dull and inert. We try to compensate by going to the theater, by reading, by watching exciting films, and by fantasying; but how much more rewarding were those brief experiences in which we became the characters on the screen or in the book—when we were the adventurers: those times of falling in love, telling someone what we really thought of him, showing physical and emotional courage, having sexual encounters, taking risks.

Too many therapists are reluctant to direct their patients toward risk. Although change, which is essential if adjustment is to be achieved, will come quickly only through courage and risk-taking, it is in the nature of our society to encourage conformity. The need to conform is also related to the nature of those who become psychotherapists. Often they have had shy and lonely childhoods, were reactors rather than actors, and preferred fantasy to deed. The training of many therapists fosters the belief that talking-it-out is "healthier" than acting-it-out, and that behaving, rather than discussing, is improper. The type of therapist who sticks with this rule would have discouraged Romeo and Juliet, preferring to make the lovers realize that they were just rebelling against their families. Today's astronauts would also be discouraged on the grounds that they are *counterphobic*—that is, "trying to prove something" not about the world but about themselves, and that this need for proof indicates hidden fear of physical danger and feelings of inferiority. Praise for adventurousness and dedication would be withheld and replaced by the old question: *Is this trip necessary?*

There is yet another irony in this attitude: Even the progress made in traditional analysis is directly related to risk-taking. For the successfully treated patient continually "risks" the exposure of his most secret wishes, feelings, and activities to another human being—his therapist.

Still, the trend in psychotherapy is, today, one of increasing tolerance of activity. People are being permitted to "do their thing" both outside and inside the therapeutic office— be it having a "freak-out" (schizophrenic break), engaging in freer sexual activities, or experiencing the impact of themselves and others in Encounter sessions.

Not surprisingly, it often develops that the insight, which the more traditional therapists were trying to evoke, came only as a follow-up to the patient's new behavior. We can get a perspective of the woods and fields and streams only after we have climbed the mountain. While we are down in the valley, the relationships remain unclear.

Verbal Reconditioning

People often restrict their activities owing to the belief that there is something terribly wrong or sinful in certain behavior. Similarly, they will try to deny their "evil" feelings. Yet what is evil to one man is often acceptable to another.

Much of this sense of which things and feelings are right and which are wrong comes from the way that natural and human responses were defined by parents in childhood.

A child who takes care of his own needs may have his behavior labeled *resourceful* by appreciative parents, and *selfish* by dependent ones. An outspoken child may be called *gutsy* or *frank* by one set of parents, or *rude and unfeeling* by a different set. A parent who defines a child's activity in a favorable way allows the child to keep, develop, and feel proud of those reactions. To define them negatively means that the child will be forced to feel guilt-ridden for having such traits, and this may lead to stultification and denial of these and many other modes of experience in later life.

Like the good parent, the therapist must demonstrate his own freedom in order to set up a followable pattern. He must also point out this "definition" process at work in the patient's life history. He must utilize these same processes actively in order to promote change. For example: A patient who stays unhappily involved with one lover and defines this as a mark of her fidelity (favorable definition) has the situation redefined by her therapist as actually being an indication of her fear of change (unfavorable definition). A woman who has many lovers and defines this as an indication of her courage and openness to sexuality (favorable) is given a redefinement: It is really an inability to tolerate involvement (unfavorable). The homosexual who prides himself on his aesthetic creativeness (favorable) is told that he is afraid of women, relationships with whom would be more creative in the truly basic sense (unfavorable). The heterosexual male who is always pleased to be in the company of women (favorable) discovers that he is "afraid of contact with men" and therefore a "latent homosexual." The result in all these cases can be a deepening of rigid behavioral patterns based on fear.

Inevitably, of any theory rooted in free and spontaneous action, the most extreme questions will be asked:

1. If the wish or need of an individual is to commit physical violence, should he, in the interests of true self-expression, be encouraged to do so?
2. Should one advocate unlimited freedom in all matters pertaining to sex? Wouldn't this lead to anarchy in marriage and deep psychological damage to the young?
3. Isn't discipline, both of the self and of others, the basis of a civilized society?

Needless to say, these are questions which trouble those who fear freedom even in its most regulated circumstances. The permissible following of impulse in Encounter groups, as well as in the therapist's office, does not include license to do permanent harm to another individual. Since freedom to express oneself is employed as a health measure, damaging violence is ruled out on the grounds that it causes illness.

As for free sexual expression for married people, could it not be said that since, in our nation, the marital relationship is among the least successful, something new is worth a try?

Concerning the young, they must be trusted as we ourselves were trusted. Perhaps we will discover the positive aspects of hippie-ism when present-day hippies have reached our stage of life. People who believe in making love (as they themselves have pointed out) do not have much energy left for making war.

In any case, the standards of free choice left to the therapeutic patient should not be underestimated. Each of us has a built-in censor: that thing which Freud called the super-ego. We tend to draw, by ourselves, limitations which are natural and "good" for us. The suffering caused in an individual who has overstepped his own bounds, or guilt-barriers, would make a second offense implausible.

"Thus conscience does make cowards of us all;
and thus the native hue of resolution
is sicklied o'er with the pale cast of thought..."

In our generation the problem is not the absence of discipline. It is instead based on the fact that (a) discipline has been misused in the past, and employed to extremes, and (b) people, even today, are being disciplined to stop thinking for themselves, to join armies, and to engage in legalized homicide.

In a society where sex and other bodily functions are looked upon with discomfort and shame, where physical intimacy with others is considered obscene, and perspiration and excreta are referred to as dirt, there is little danger of driving the average individual to an excess of freedom.

There are two sides to the coin of mental health. One involves a continuous effort on the part of the individual to understand and eliminate his disruptive reactions (hatred, jealousy, smoldering resentment) and the behavior which springs from them. The other involves an acceptance of self as imperfect, without shame and self-blame for our human reactions.

We have gone into the ways in which therapists can help their patients to reach this end. It is no easy goal to achieve. We all deceive ourselves and our patients much of the time. In place of respect for the patient's autonomy, we seek to impose our wills, to control. In place of frankly acknowledging our own emotional responses, we tend to hide or deny them behind masks of neutrality. Instead of working to promote change, and making the patient aware of the tasks he must set for himself, we play intellectual and therapeutic Games.

Our hope lies in honesty—a trait revered in others, but fearsome to contemplate within ourselves. To be honest bears consequences: disapproval, criticism, rejection. The friend who tells the truth is open to the loss of friendship. The human being who *is* the truth, who is himself and lives by his own standards at any cost, is often met with opposition. Yet honesty is the only workable basis for any real relationship.

The traditional pretense, or game structure, in much therapy today, is, although safe in its wide professional acceptance, the brick wall between treatment and resolution. With further education and self-searching, we must grow—so that one day we may discover the wasteful overarmament in our human psyches. It will be with this realization that we drop our ironclad defenses, to find that there is little need for our crippling fears after all.